A Sweet Dash of Aloha

A *Sweet* Dash of Aloha

Guilt-Free Hawai'i Desserts and Snacks

KAPI'OLANI COMMUNITY COLLEGE
University of Hawai'i

This book was made possible by grants from the United States Department of Agriculture and the Hawai'i State Department of Agriculture. The authors would also like to express their gratitude to Whole Foods Kahala for its enthusiastic and generous support in the development of recipes and content for this book.

© 2011 Kapi'olani Community College, University of Hawai'i
Kapi'olani Community College is an
Equal Opportunity/Affirmative Action Institution

All rights reserved. No part of this book may be reproduced in any form or by any electronic or mechanical means, including information retrieval systems, without prior written permission from the publisher, except for brief passages quoted in reviews.

ISBN: 978-1-9358901-2-2

Library of Congress Control Number:
2011939910

Culinary photography
Adriana Torres Chong

Photographs pp. vi, 4, 10, 18
David Croxford, HAWAI'I Magazine

Design and production
Gonzalez Design Company

Watermark Publishing
1088 Bishop Street, Suite 310
Honolulu, Hawai'i 96813
Telephone 1-808-587-7766
Toll-free 1-866-900-BOOK
sales@bookshawaii.net
www.bookshawaii.net

Printed in China

CONTENTS

1	**Foreword**
4	**Chapter 1** Eating Pono: The What, How and Why of Healthful Treats and Snacks
10	**Chapter 2** Eat Sweets—and Stay Heart-Healthy Too
16	**A Guide to Ingredients**
18	**Chapter 3** Taking Care: Ola and Diabetes
22	**Chapter 4** How Sweet It Is—without Refined Sugar
44	**Chapter 5** Egg 'Em On—with Egg Alternatives
56	**Chapter 6** The Staff of Life: Baking Healthful Bread
74	**Chapter 7** Gluten Gone
98	**Chapter 8** Have Your Cake and Eat It Too
108	**Chapter 9** It's a Jungle Out There: Cooking with Island Fruit
124	**Chapter 10** Sweet Child of Mine: Family-Friendly Treats
156	**Chapter 11** The Outer Limits
174	**Hawai'i Nutrition & Seasonality Charts**
180	**Contributors**
185	**Index**

FOREWORD

By Dr. Laurie Steelsmith, N.D., L.Ac.

Confronted with chocolate, our thoughts race. Every warning about sweets, fats, desserts and, yes, decadent chocolate rings in our ears. Doctors, mothers, classmates, friends and even casual acquaintances have weighed in on how our heart, thighs, calves, tummy and other body parts will be compromised by such indulgences. We sigh and turn away. Or we bite into that piece of chocolate cake anyway and then are weighed down by guilt.

This dilemma isn't hard to understand: We're programmed to want sugar. Our brains use 60 percent of our body's glucose, the simplest sugar in the body, for metabolic activity. And our cells need sugar to create energy. But there are different kinds of sugars, some far better for us than others.

For every one of us caught up in the incessant progression of sugar spikes and blues, this book offers alternatives. These pages include an expansive selection of healthy, heart-conscious and body-conscious snacks and sweets that won't wreck your physical and mental state. They offer an array of ways to substitute "good" sugars for "bad" ones, "good" fats for "bad" ones, whole grains for processed ones, providing recipes for treats made with wholesome fruits, nuts and even vegetables, many grown here in Hawai'i.

If sweets without guilt are your goal, it's important to start with an understanding of the differences in sugars and how they react in the body. Simple sugars such as refined white sugar are converted most quickly to energy, potentially creating sugar "highs" and "lows"—spikes of quick energy followed by plummeting sugar "blues." Complex sugars from fruits and vegetables, however, offer a slower, more even release of energy. Slow-moving complex sugars help keep blood sugar levels normal and prevent mood swings or feelings of agitation.

Alternatives are the reason for this book: to suggest a range of substitutes for refined sugar, whole eggs, glutinous and low-fiber flours and other less healthful ingredients and cooking techniques common to the American diet.

Take, for example, healthy complex sugars low on the glycemic index. The glycemic index is a measure of how quickly a carbohydrate is converted to sugar. If a carbohydrate converts slowly to a simple sugar in your body, that means it will provide an evenly spaced supply of energy. If it converts quickly, you will experience a rapid rise in blood sugar followed by a dramatic drop, resulting in unpleasant symptoms such as mood swings, anxiety and sugar cravings.

There's more: Not only do these easy, low-glycemic, nutritious substitutions create overall health and well-being, they help you to maintain a less-stressed and more protective immune system. And they can be a front line of defense against disease or other medical issues, including weight gain, or the increasingly widespread and serious problems of heart disease, atherosclerosis and diabetes. For example, using rich and healthy avocado to moisten a chocolate pudding pie won't create either a surge of guilt or a spike in blood sugar.

Flours made from coconut, tapioca, potato, hazelnuts, pecans, garbanzo beans, almonds, soybeans or sorghum instead of wheat, barley and rye remove the gluten. In some people, gluten stimulates a range of uncomfortable symptoms from joint pain and inflammation to skin rashes and fatigue. If you have gluten intolerance, it may seem that baked goods would be off limits for you, but you can still enjoy delicious treats without the severe side effects.

You may think it can't be as easy as it sounds: Just opt for alternatives. But it is. Here are three ways to help you begin making choices that will allow you to enjoy satisfying sweets and snacks without the downsides.

- Make a decision. You must believe that you need to change and you must want the results of change more than the comfort of your old ways. For some of us, it's a decision to begin loving ourselves. Too often in our lives we beat ourselves up…"Oh, I shouldn't have eaten that"…"Why am I so undisciplined?"… "Why can't I do what Susie does…?" Sometimes this negative thinking is so ingrained we hardly recognize it. We feel bad about ourselves, captured by an internal dialogue that's been instilled somewhere along the line, often wrongfully and harshly. That cycle can be stopped. Instead of coming at yourself with anger and annoyance, come to yourself with kindness and affection. You're lovable. You're gorgeous, or you're a hunk. Your humor is infectious, your compassion boundless. As you change the internal dialogue, you will get to a place where you love yourself enough to take care of yourself. Your body. Your spirit. Those chubby thighs. It's all about being okay with the you that you are now. You don't have to wait until you graduate, or get married, or earn that Ph.D. You can change right now, as you are at this very minute. Recognize that loving yourself doesn't mean you have to live a spartan life. Or a life without joy. You can recognize that tasty food is good for you, and it's a joyful thing. But it needs to be healthy and vital food to create a healthy and vital life.

- Know that you are not defined by your body. When you understand and embrace this idea, you can take care of yourself as your primary process. That means not accepting self-defeating thoughts but changing those thoughts to "I want to take care of me"…"I want to love me." By changing your head, heart and spirit, anything is possible. Nothing feels too hard, too expensive or too impossible.

- Finally, you need to master the specifics of how to change: the elements of a healthy diet, the techniques for cutting back on unhealthful ingredients. That's where this book comes in. It will enable you to translate your decision in favor of positive change into seamless action. That action can be as easy as walking past the processed flour and sugar at the grocery store, picking up a package of dates and a jar of raw macadamia nuts instead.

For example, chocolate pudding pie can be made with avocado and refined coconut oil for moistness, dates and maple syrup for sweetening, and raw macadamia nuts for crunch. I was offered a slice after a cooking demonstration; the taste and texture are unbelievable. I couldn't stop thinking about it for days afterwards! So many people believe that healthy foods can't taste good, or are too difficult to make. In this book, you'll discover that these are the same kinds of myths that have kept you from changing until this moment. Local health food stores are now well supplied with all of these alternatives, and mainstream grocery stores are also beginning to understand the importance of these healthy choices. You will eat well; the flavors will be fantastic and the cooking generally easy. You've got nothing to lose but your health problems and risks. You could even start today.

Dr. Laurie Steelsmith is a licensed naturopathic physician and acupuncturist and the author of the Hawai'i best-selling book Natural Choices for Women's Health *(Three Rivers/Random House).*

CHAPTER ONE

Eating Pono: The What, How and Why of Healthful Treats and Snacks

By Daniel Leung, M.S.W.,
A.S. (Culinary Arts), Educational Specialist

Grant Itomitsu, Registered Dietitian, Nutrition Instructor
Kapiʻolani Community College

Pono, in the Hawaiian language, means righteous, correct and good. For this book, eating pono means eating well and eating healthily. We believe that all foods are meant to be eaten. And there is no such thing as "bad" food in nature. For example, sugar is not your enemy. Sugar is energy for the human body. It occurs in an enormous variety of foods. We naturally crave sweetness, as it indicates good energy sources. When it comes to health, though, it is how you consume sugar, what forms of sweeteners you use and how much you eat that are at issue. So, we are not here to tell you not to enjoy sweet things (or, for that matter, foods that contain certain fats, starches or proteins). Our goal is to show you how to enjoy your treats while maintaining good health.

"What can we enjoy?" you may ask. Continuing with sugar as the example, what to do about all this talk of sugar being unhealthy? The varieties of sugars to be concerned about are highly refined sugars, mostly added to food when it is cooked (as in desserts, snack treats and savory dishes); baked (cakes, pastries); or manufactured (processed foods). The highest quality source of sweetness comes from natural ingredients in their least processed form: fruits and vegetables.

This book will show you how to make use of some of the best produce from Hawai'i's farms, adding great flavors and sweetness to desserts and treats. In Hawai'i's gentle climate, our farmers are able to grow a wide variety of colorful and tasty tropical fruits that can provide you with the nutrition that your body needs. We can eat a rainbow of incredible flavors including lichee, dragon fruit, rambutan, longan or "dragon eye," mangosteen and much more, in addition to the commonly known pineapple, mango, papaya, banana and starfruit. Interesting to note, the more vibrant the color, the more cancer-fighting antioxidants are present in the produce. Fresh fruits and vegetables also contain healthy fibers essential for our digestive systems and the prevention of colon cancer.

"How do we eat well and eat for health?" The key words are "balance" and "moderation." By nature, we all need sugar. It is the source of energy for our brains and our bodies. A lack of sugar affects our emotional well-being. All of us have experienced being cranky and irritable when we are hungry—when we have low blood sugar levels. Even if we do not ingest plain sugar, other foods can be converted into sugar to meet our energy needs, such as starch or carbohydrates (for example, pasta, rice and potatoes). But not all of us convert sugar to useful energy at the same rate. This partly depends on your rate of metabolism and partly on your energy output—how physically active a lifestyle you live. This is the simple concept of "energy balance": The more physically active you are, the more energy, and hence nutrients—including sugar and fat—you will use up.

Childhood obesity is now a major concern for Hawai'i and the rest of the United States. It is partly a result of taking in too much sugar from unhealthy sources such as soda, candy and processed foods. We also are not consuming enough fresh fruits and vegetables, from which we derive healthy sugars plus all the goodness that comes with them—vitamins, minerals and fiber. In addition, children and many adults are leading dramatically more sedentary lives, spending more time sitting in front of computers and televisions than in playing sports or being physically active.

An expert committee convened by the American Medical Association, the State of Hawai'i Department of Health and Human Service's Health Resources and Service Administration, and the Center for Disease Control offers an easy formula for healthy eating, aimed at children and youth, but not a bad idea for adults either: "5-2-1-almost none" (or 5-2-1-0). The numbers refer to recommended daily practices: eating a minimum of 5 servings of fruits and vegetables daily, engaging in not more than 2 hours of "screen time" (television, computer, video games, etc.) daily and at least 1 hour of physical activity daily, and avoiding sugary drinks and other highly refined, sugar-packed products.

Dr. May Okihiro, director of the Hawaii Initiative for Childhood Obesity Research and Education, explains that sugary drinks such as soda, sweetened tea, sports drinks, fruit punch and other fruit-flavored drinks have little nutritional benefit. Sweetened beverages add empty calories, about 150 calories and 9 teaspoons of sugar per 12-oz. can of soda. Water is one of our most important nutrients. Encourage your family to love water. Serve it. Choose it. If it's all that's offered, people will drink it. Try enlivening plain water with fresh herbs such as chopped mint or lemon verbena, or with slices of fruit, such as Kāʻū oranges or local limes. Don't be swayed by advertising. Juice products labeled "drink" or "punch," or ending in "-ade" (such as orangeade) usually contain mostly corn syrup sweetener and very little real juice. If you do serve juice, choose 100-percent fruit juice, cut it with water (by one third or more) and try to limit such treats to less than a cup a day.

Using fresh and dried fruits to sweeten desserts, baked goods and snacks adds layers of flavor and texture in addition to natural sugars. The natural tanginess (acid) in many fruits excites our palates. For example, a squeeze of lime juice on fresh papaya yields a totally different, more refreshing experience. This book offers plenty of exciting and practical ideas on how to incorporate nature's sweetness into your daily life without excess sugar.

For people who have special dietary restrictions on their intake of sugar or gluten, we have created many recipes to allow you to enjoy sweet treats and baked goods while maintaining your health. We believe in providing options, not setting restrictions.

Why should we use local fruits and vegetables? The answer is simple: Better quality and freshness equals better nutrition and flavor. The simplest way to determine freshness is to think of the time and distance it took for that particular piece of produce to travel from the farm to your table. The shorter the distance, the less time it takes, the fresher it is likely to be. Fruits and vegetables from Hawaiʻi farms are usually not more than a few hours away. From farm to table, they come via roads or airfreight between islands, then are delivered to warehouses and then to market. Local produce from farmer's markets is likely to have been harvested mere hours from sale. Compare that to imported items, which are picked before peak ripeness so they will travel better, transported via truck and train, then sit in warehouses and docks for several days prior to the oversea journey on boats taking weeks, finally reaching Hawai'i's ports, only to await inspection and further distribution. But Island farmers can wait for produce to ripen in the fields and plant varieties that favor flavor over longevity. Imported foods may or may not ripen during transport. Fruits that are allowed to ripen naturally definitely have better taste and texture and better retain their nutritional value. Why not use what is best for you, support our farmers and keep Hawai'i green at the same time?

"Lucky we live Hawai'i!" is a popular local expression. Lucky indeed, as we can have our desserts and treats and enjoy good health because of hard work and the aloha that our farmers put into their produce. Add a dash of fresh, Hawaiian sweetness from the 'āina. And that's all you need to eat pono.

CHAPTER TWO

Eat Sweets—
and Stay Heart-Healthy Too

By Dr. Stephen Bradley
Metro Oʻahu Board of Directors,
American Heart Association

The term "nutritious" placed in front of the word "sweets" may seem like an oxymoron. However, it is possible to include an occasional delectable treat in your diet while maintaining your cardiovascular health so long as you keep one eye on the total amount of fat, saturated fat and calories you eat. The real trick is to track and balance your food intake throughout the entire week and choose only desserts that fit in with your plan for good health. The American Heart Association offers a helpful tool called "My Life Check" to help you develop a plan for good health (www.mylifecheck.org).

The American Heart Association's Nutrition Committee strongly advises that these fat guidelines be followed by healthy Americans over the age of two:
- Limit total fat intake to less than 25–35 percent of total calorie intake each day;
- Limit saturated fat intake to less than 7 percent of total daily calories;
- Limit trans-fat intake to less than 1 percent of total daily calories;
- Remaining fat should come from sources of monounsaturated and polyunsaturated fats such as nuts, seeds, fish and vegetable oils; and
- Limit cholesterol intake to less than 300 mg per day. But if you have coronary heart disease or an LDL cholesterol level of 100 mg/dL or greater, limit cholesterol intake to less than 200 milligrams a day.

Saturated Fat
Saturated fat is the main dietary cause of high blood cholesterol. Saturated fat is found mostly in foods from animals, but from some plant sources as well. In desserts, saturated fats most often come in the form of lard, butter, cream, milk, cheeses and other dairy products made from whole and 2-percent milk. All of these foods also contain dietary cholesterol. Plants that contain saturated fat include coconut, coconut oil, palm oil, palm kernel oil (often called tropical oils) and cocoa butter.

Trans-Fats and Hydrogenated Fats
Trans-fats are formed during the process of hydrogenation, a technique used in making margarine, shortening and cooking oils. Foods made with these are a major source of trans-fats in the American diet. In clinical studies, trans-fat tended to raise total blood cholesterol levels. Some scientists believe the trans-

fats raise cholesterol levels more than saturated fats. Trans-fats also tend to raise LDL (bad) cholesterol and lower HDL (good) cholesterol, raising the risk of heart disease.

Recent studies on the potential cholesterol-raising effects of trans-fats have raised public concern about the use of conventional margarine and whether other options, including butter, might be a better choice. Some stick margarines contribute more trans-fats than unhydrogenated oils or other fats.

Because butter is rich in both saturated fat and cholesterol, it's potentially a highly atherogenic food (a food that causes the arteries to be blocked). Most margarine is made from vegetable fat and provides no dietary cholesterol. The more liquid the margarine—such as those sold in tubs or squeezable plastic bottles—the less hydrogenated it is and the less trans-fat it contains.

The trans-fat content of foods is printed on the package on the Nutrition Facts label. Keep trans-fat intake to less than 1 percent of total calories. For example, if you need 2,000 calories a day, you should consume less than 2 grams of trans-fat.

Polyunsaturated Fat
Polyunsaturated and monounsaturated fats are the two unsaturated fats. Some examples of foods used in desserts that contain these fats include walnuts and liquid vegetable oils such as soybean, corn, safflower, canola and sunflower.

Both polyunsaturated and monounsaturated fats may help lower your blood cholesterol level when you use them in place of saturated and trans-fats.

Too Much Sugar Isn't So Sweet for Your Health
Many people consume more sugar than they realize. There are two types of sugars in American diets: naturally occurring sugars and added sugars.

- Naturally occurring sugars such as fructose (fruit sugars) and lactose (milk sugars) are found in those foods just as they come, rather than being added during processing.
- Added sugars are just that: sugars or caloric sweeteners added to food or beverages during processing or preparation (such as putting sugar in your coffee or adding sugar to your cereal). These may include natural products such as white or brown sugar and honey as well as caloric sweeteners that are chemically manufactured (such as high fructose corn syrup).

Added sugars contribute zero nutrients but many added calories that can lead to extra pounds or even obesity, thereby reducing heart health.

If you think of your daily calorie needs as a budget, you want to "spend" most of your calories on "essentials" to meet your nutrient needs. Use only leftover, discretionary calories for "extras" that provide little or no nutritional benefit, such as sugar. There are four calories in each gram of sugar, so if a product has 15 grams of sugar per serving, that's 60 calories just from the sugar alone.

The American Heart Association (AHA) recommends limiting the amount of added sugars you consume to no more than half of your daily discretionary calories allowance. For most American women, that's no more than 100 calories per day, or about 6 teaspoons of sugar. For men, it's 150 calories per day, or about 9 teaspoons.

Tips for Lowering Sugar in Desserts
- Cut the sugar called for in cookies, brownies or cakes by one-third to one-half. Often you won't notice the difference and it won't affect the success of the recipe.
- Use extracts such as almond, vanilla, orange or lemon to incorporate flavor without sweetening.
- Enhance foods with spices instead of sugar; try ginger, allspice, cinnamon or nutmeg or more exotic additions such as cardamom, sea salt flakes or cayenne.
- Substitute unsweetened applesauce measure for measure for sugar in forgiving recipes such as quick breads and bar cookies; you may need to reduce liquid in recipe.

- Use non-nutritive sweeteners such as aspartame or sucralose in moderation. Non-nutritive sweeteners may be a way to satisfy your sweet tooth without adding more calories to your diet. The FDA has determined that some non-nutritive sweeteners are safe.

The American Heart Association has declared obesity a major risk factor for heart disease. Obesity also increases the risk of diabetes, which can in turn lead to heart disease.

Eating healthy doesn't mean you can't occasionally eat dessert. But it's important to ration treats to every few days and make sure they're low in saturated fats and added sugars. As well, watching calories is key, since maintaining a healthful weight is important to heart health.

A Guide to Ingredients

Following is a listing of ingredients, including definitions and resources, used in the recipes in this book. You'll also find sugar alternatives in Chapter 2, egg alternatives in Chapter 3 and flour alternatives in Chapter 5.

- Agar-agar, aka kanten: A gelatin-like substance made from algae, used for thickening. Asian grocers or in Asian grocery section; health food stores.

- Almond milk: "Milk" extracted from blanched ground almonds by means of hot water; low cholesterol, no lactose. Health food stores and some groceries.

- Azuki beans: Small, slow-cooking, low-fat, high-protein beans used in many Japanese confections in a paste form; canned in smooth (koshian) and chunky (tsubushian) forms. Asian grocers or in Asian grocery section.

- Coconut oil, refined and unrefined: Coconut oil responds well to high heat without breaking down (oxidizing). Coconut oil is said to have significant health benefits despite its high saturated fat content. It is not stored as fat but used as energy; does not cause an insulin spike as do regular carbohydrates; and contains lauric acid, which converts to monolaurin, a fatty acid with antiviral, anti-fungal and anti-bacterial properties. Refined coconut oil or pure coconut oil is made from copra (dried or smoked coconut meat), processed to remove impurities and coconut flavor and aroma. Therefore, it is favored for culinary uses where coconut flavor is not desired. Unrefined, virgin or raw oil is extracted from fresh, unprocessed, grated and pressed coconut meat. It is fragrant and tastes like sweet, fresh coconut. Store coconut oil in a cool, dark environment; it will solidify below 76 degrees. Health food stores. More information: www.spectrumorganics.com; www.coconotoil.com/maryenig.htm; www.naturalchoicesforwomen.com; www.mercola.com

- Couscous: Pasta-like dried granules of semolina wheat dough, usually served steamed but also used in baked goods. Widely available.

- Lemon verbena: An herb (*Aloysia citrodora*) much appreciated by the French (who call it verveine) with an intense citrusy flavor in the delicate leaves. Grows well in Island gardens (even in pots). Farmer's markets and herb vendors.

- Margarine: Both butter and margarine yield about 35 calories per teaspoon, but some margarine is about 25 percent fat as compared to butter's 80 percent. Margarine is made from plant sources and so is low in saturated fat and contains no dietary cholesterol. But because stick margarine is hardened through a process called hydrogenation, it is high in trans-fats, which may raise levels of bad cholesterol and lower levels of good cholesterol. Preferable—and used throughout this book—are light spreads, the soft, spreadable margarine found in plastic tubs. Named best vegan spread by about.com, Earth Balance Natural Spread was used in testing many of these recipes. Earth Balance spreads—there are a number of types and flavors—are free of trans-fats, hydrogenated oils and artificial ingredients. Tastes buttery and can be used wherever butter is called for. Health food stores and some groceries.

- Medjool or medjul dates: A fruit harvested from date palms, considered to be exceptionally good quality. Widely available.

- Mochiko: Sweet rice flour. Used for steamed, boiled and baked Asian-style sweets, such as mochi cakes, chichidango and butter mochi. Asian groceries or in Oriental grocery section.

- Mung bean threads (aka long rice, saifun, cellophane noodles): Clear, thin dried Chinese noodles made from mung beans; reconstitute briefly in warm or hot water. Widely available in grocers' Asian foods section.

- Protein powder: Lowfat, high-protein powder made from eggs, whey (a cheese by-product), soy and other sources. Nutrition supply and bodybuilding stores.

- Tahini: Sesame seed butter, a rich, smooth oily spread and ingredient in such recipes as salad dressings, hummous and baked goods. Widely available.

- Xanthan gum and guar gum: Common, natural thickening and emulsifying agents. Xanthan gum is a fermented corn or cabbage sugar product. Guar gum is a product of the guar plant, grown in Pakistan and northern India; it is made from the dried and split seeds. These gums replace eggs and dairy ingredients in vegan recipes and dishes for people with food allergies or sensitivities. A very small amount of these ingredients has powerful gelling qualities. Health food stores.

- Zest: The finely grated outer peel of citrus fruit, preferably without the bitter pith (white lining). A rasp-style grater is best for harvesting zest. *Zest* is both a noun and a verb.

CHAPTER THREE

Taking Care:
Ola and Diabetes

Cyndy Kahalewale, MPH, RD
Nutrition Lecturer and Renal Dietitian
Kapiʻolani Community College

Ola, in the Hawaiian language, means life, health, well-being and thriving. Each and every one of us strives for ola. One of our biggest public health problems today is diabetes mellitus, or simply, diabetes. If we don't have it, we know someone who does, and many of us have family members with the disease. We see the complications that arise from diabetes. Many people accept this as a natural part of life. Some would say, "This is part of the problem." The disease is so prevalent; many people may feel there is nothing we can do. Is there? Yes, there is plenty we can do. We must start by learning what to do to prevent diabetes from occurring. And, if someone is diagnosed with the disease, the best weapon is to learn how to manage it with diet and lifestyle changes. Following are some of the common myths associated with diabetes.

Myth #1
Diabetes is not a serious disease.
In fact, diabetes causes more deaths per year than breast cancer and AIDS combined. One out of every third child born in or after the year 2000 will be directly affected by diabetes. (In Hawai'i, it is thought that one out of every two children will be affected).

Myth #2
Diabetes is caused by eating too much sugar.
Diabetes is hereditary. It can also be caused by lifestyle factors such as being overweight. People who are overweight usually are consuming more energy in the form of calories than the energy they are burning. A high-calorie diet typically consists of high-fat foods. Many of these high-fat foods can also have a significant amount of sugar.

Myth #3
People with diabetes should eat special diabetic foods.
It is recommended that people with diabetes eat a healthy diet—the same diet we all should be eating. This diet should be low in fat, with moderate amounts of salt and sugar. This diet should include whole grains and a good variety of fresh fruits and vegetables. There is no special benefit from eating "diabetic" or "dietetic" foods.

Myth #4
People with diabetes can't eat sweets or chocolate.
If eaten as part of a healthy diet overall, sweets and desserts can be eaten by

people with diabetes. This is the same recommendation as for people without it.

Myth #5
It is better for people with diabetes to eat natural sugars like honey and agave—as long as they stay away from white sugar.
Although there are health benefits to eating more "natural" forms of sugar such as honey and agave, there is no significant health benefit in avoiding white sugar when trying to control diabetes. What's more important is to modify the total amount of carbohydrate in the diet: eating healthier choices such as whole grains and natural forms of sugar—including fresh fruits.

Clearly, there are many misconceptions about diet and diabetes. Once someone is diagnosed with diabetes, they should continue to try and eat a healthy diet, the same diet many of us without diabetes work at every day. So, what is a healthy diet? Once you sit down to eat, take a moment to look at your plate. If it is a healthy meal, it is most desirable to have half your plate filled with fresh fruits and vegetables. The other half of the plate can be split between foods high in protein and foods made of carbohydrates.
Tip: If you have diabetes and want a sweet treat after your meal, save some of your carbohydrate allowance on your meal plate for that treat and enjoy. In other words, if you want to have a dessert or special treat, eat less carbohydrate at mealtime.

Achieving and maintaining a healthy weight is also very important in preventing the onset of diabetes. The best way to keep your weight within a healthy range is to choose foods lower in fat and lower in total calories. Along with exercise, this can help you in your efforts to stay at a healthy weight. Eating lower-fat foods and foods lower in calories can easily be done by increasing your portions of fresh fruits and vegetables. We in Hawai'i have so many choices of locally grown fresh fruits and vegetables. We hope this cookbook will suggest a variety of options to try—at least once.

Komo mai kau mapuna hoe
"Dip your paddle in."
Join in the effort.

Pae mai la ka wa'a i ka 'āina
"The canoe has come ashore"
Hunger is satisfied; desire fulfilled.

—Mary Kawena Pukui, *'Olelo No'eau*

CHAPTER FOUR

How Sweet It Is— without Refined Sugar

Alternative sweeteners—whether in a dry form that mimics granulated sugar, as a liquid or in the form of fruit or natural syrups—can mean taking in fewer calories, avoiding the energy spikes and sudden drops common with refined sugar and yet satisfying a craving for sweets. Here are examples ranging from candies to cookies, Asian rice cakes to pies.

Alternative Sweeteners

Following are the alternative sweeteners that are the most widely available and the best understood.

- Agave syrup is a mild-tasting syrup that comes from a cactus-like plant. It has a light honey- or maple syrup-like flavor. Health food stores, some grocers.

- Barley malt is made from roasted barley sprouts. It is not as sweet as honey. It works well in most baked goods.

- Brown rice syrup is a mild-flavored sweetener made from rice starch. Use it wherever you would normally use honey or other liquid sweeteners. Try it in hot and cold drinks or as a topping for pancakes, waffles and desserts. Rice syrup is very thick, so it does not work as well as other liquid sweeteners for baking. Find it at health food stores.

- Dates are high in vitamins and minerals as well as sugar, and they contain quite a bit of fiber. Blend them into pancake, waffle or other batters, or chop them to sweeten cookies, cakes and raw desserts. Or enjoy dates on their own as a dessert nibble. Medjool dates are especially favored for eating solo. Buy dates seed-in or seeded; prepared chopped dates may be coated with dextrose or other ingredients to prevent sticking. To prevent them from clumping in dishes such as quick bread recipes, toss them in flour after chopping or processing. Grocers and health food stores.

- Date sugar is a nutritious sweetener made from dehydrated dates that are ground up into a powder. It makes a great substitute for sugar in most things except for beverages (it does not dissolve well). Use ⅔ to 1 cup of date sugar in place of 1 cup white sugar. Health food stores.

- Use fresh fruit as a natural sweetener. Here are some ideas: Use in place of sugar to sweeten breakfast cereal or porridge. Try mashed bananas, fresh apple purée (or even applesauce) to sweeten and add moisture to quick breads, muffins and cookies.

- Fruit juices may replace some or all of the liquid ingredients in baked goods such as muffins, breads, cakes and cookies. Fruit juices are also good for sweetening sweet sauces, homemade Popsicles and fruit salads; apple or grape juice can replace wine in savory sauces. You can even use frozen fruit juice concentrates. Or make your own by slowly cooking fruit juice (white grape, apple, orange or pineapple juice) until it has been reduced by one quarter.

- Natural honey is very good for you. It's high in vitamins and minerals (such as B_2, B_6 and iron) and has antioxidant and antibacterial properties. Pasteurized commercial honey does not have these benefits. So be sure to choose raw honey that is minimally filtered. Use ½ to ¾ cup of raw honey to replace 1 cup of sugar. To substitute honey for white or brown sugar in baked goods, reduce the liquid by ¼ cup and lower the baking temperature by 25 degrees.

- Maple syrup is the concentrated sap from the sugar maple tree. It is high in calcium and contains other nutrients. Non-organic maple syrup may contain unwanted additives, so choose organic maple syrup. Use maple syrup to replace honey or sugar in recipes. Choose it for pancakes and waffles instead of the artificial stuff. Use ½ to ¾ cup maple syrup to replace 1 cup of sugar. Health food stores and grocers.

- Maple sugar is made by evaporating maple syrup. It is twice as sweet as white sugar, so use only ½ cup maple sugar to replace 1 cup of sugar. Health food stores and grocers.

- Molasses is a mineral-rich sweetener high in calcium, iron and potassium. It is the product that remains when sugar crystals are separated from sugar cane syrup. Choose unsulfured molasses. Widely available.

- Splenda is a non-caloric sweetener made from sucralose (sucralose is sugar that's been treated with a laundry list of chemicals). In its granulated form, it sweetens cup for cup like sugar, without the aftertaste of many other sweeteners. It's sold in bags and boxes like sugar. Some people have experienced digestive upset when consuming Splenda; introduce it cautiously. Splenda Brown Sugar blend is half Splenda and half brown sugar. Information: http://www.splenda.com/cooking-baking/conversion-charts

- Stevia is a natural sweetener made from a non-caloric herb well known to the Guarani people of Paraguay (they called it kaa he-he, "sweet herb"). It is about 30 times sweeter than sugar, so you use it by the drop. A little goes a very long way. It's great for sweetening beverages and some desserts. Stevia does have a unique taste, so it doesn't work for everything. Health food stores (in the nutritional supplements department in eye dropper-style bottles) and online. See www.stevia.net

- Sucanat is a dry sweetener made by dehydrating organic sugar cane juice. It is more nutritious and flavorful than white sugar because the molasses has not been removed. It works very well for baked goods and in other dishes that call for white sugar. It does add a bit of color due to the molasses content, so you may not want to use it in dishes where a lighter color is important. Use it cup for cup to replace white or brown sugar. Health food stores.

- Truvia is a blend of stevia and erythritol, a sugar alcohol that has been found not to upset the digestive system in the manner of other sugar alcohols (i.e., maltitol, sorbitol, xylitol). It is granular like sugar and sold in packets. Ratios: 1 tsp. sugar = ⅜ tsp. (half a packet) Truvia; 1 T. = 1¼ tsp. Truvia (1½ packets); ¼ cup sugar= 1 T. plus 2 tsp. Truvia (6 packets); 1 cup= ⅓ cup plus 1 T (24 packets). Information: www.Truvia.com

Remember: Using alternative sweeteners isn't a license to pour it on. Moderate use of all forms of sugar and sugar substitutes helps wean your palate away from oversweet foods and your brain away from sugar cravings. And some forms of sweetener may be difficult for sensitive stomachs to digest. Easy does it.

— Alyssa Moreau

Chocolate-Dipped Macaroons

Makes 20 cookies *Alyssa Moreau*

No refined sugar in these, except for what's in the indulgent dark chocolate in which these chewy cookies are dipped. Silken tofu adds protein and moisture; it can be found by the fresh refrigerated tofu (sold fresh) or in an aseptic box on the shelf in the Asian section of the grocery store.

1 c.	brown rice flour
1½ c.	shredded unsweetened coconut
10 pckt.	Truvia
1 tsp.	baking powder
½ tsp.	salt
¼ c.	silken tofu
3 T.	light oil (such as coconut, high-oleic safflower, grapeseed, canola)
¼ c.	almond milk
1 tsp.	vanilla
2 tsp.	almond extract
½ c.	dark chocolate

Preheat oven to 350 degrees. Line a baking sheet with parchment paper. In a large mixing bowl, combine the dry ingredients. Blend together the liquid ingredients (an immersion blender works well); add to dry mixture. Drop by tablespoonfuls onto prepared baking sheet and bake 14 minutes (check at 12 minutes) or until nicely browned on the bottoms and edges. Cool on baking rack. Melt chocolate on stove or in microwave. Dip cookies partway into chocolate. Cool cookies and store in refrigerator or freezer until serving time.

Variations:
- Instead of Truvia, you can use ⅓ cup agave, honey or other liquid sweetener; omit almond milk.
- Substitute whole wheat pastry flour for brown rice flour.
- Omit chocolate or add chocolate chips to dough.

Nutrition Facts
Serving Size (32g)
Servings Per Container

Amount Per Serving

Calories 120   Calories from Fat 70

% Daily Value*

Total Fat 8g	12%
Saturated Fat 4.5g	23%
Trans Fat 0g	
Cholesterol 0mg	0%
Sodium 90mg	4%
Total Carbohydrate 12g	4%
Dietary Fiber 1g	4%
Sugars 3g	
Protein 2g	

Almond Panna Cotta with Tropical Fruit Confetti

Makes 6 servings *Stephen Bradley*

This lower-fat version of a molto fashionable Italian dessert is courtesy of Dr. Stephen Bradley of the American Heart Association.

1	envelope unflavored gelatin
½ c.	cold water
⅔ c.	(2-percent) milk
¼ c. + 2 T.	Sucanat (made from natural cane sugar)
2 T.	Amaretto liqueur
1 tsp.	almond extract
1 lb.	assorted tropical fruits
1 T.	orange liqueur (Cointreau or Grand Marnier)

For the panna cotta: In a small saucepan, sprinkle the envelope of gelatin over the cold water and let stand for 3 minutes to soften ("bloom"). Heat the mixture over medium heat, stirring, until dissolved. Stir in the milk and ¼ cup Sucanat; heat until milk is just hot and Sucanat dissolved. Remove from heat. Add the Amaretto and almond extract and pour into 6 (6-ounce) ramekins. Cover and refrigerate overnight; at least 6-8 hours.

For the fruit confetti: Choose 1 pound of local tropical fruits with a variety of tastes and textures (e.g., mango, lychee, firm papaya, starfruit, guava, mangosteen, dragonfruit) and carefully cut into small cubes of even size. Mix with the remaining 2 T. of Sucanat and 1 T. orange liqueur. Allow to stand for at least 15 minutes.

Scatter 2 tablespoons fruit confetti over a dessert plate, reserving some for garnish. Place each ramekin in warm water for a minute and run a flexible, thin-bladed knife around the edge to loosen panna cotta. Invert and unmold panna cotta on top of confetti. Spoon a small amount of the sauce (the sweetened juices and liqueur from the fruit bowl) over the panna cotta. Top with a final sprinkle of the confetti.

Nutrition Facts

Serving Size (224g)
Servings Per Container

Amount Per Serving

Calories 220   Calories from Fat 15

% Daily Value*

Total Fat 2g	3%
Saturated Fat 1g	5%
Trans Fat 0g	
Cholesterol 10mg	3%
Sodium 80mg	3%
Total Carbohydrate 32g	11%
Dietary Fiber 1g	4%
Sugars 28g	
Protein 16g	

Bliss Balls

Makes 10-12 balls *Alyssa Moreau*

These no-cook treats are so versatile: Incorporate different dried fruits, chocolate or other chips or nut butters to create a personalized blissful ball of your own.

½ c.	almond butter
½ c.	tahini (sesame butter)
½ c.	mashed ripe banana
1 tsp.	vanilla
¼ c.	carob powder (sifted) or cocoa or cacao powder
½ c.	fresh or dried shredded unsweetened coconut
4-5 pckt.	Truvia
½ tsp.	cinnamon
¼ tsp.	nutmeg
¼ tsp.	ginger
2-4 T.	raisins
	Pinch salt

Combine first 4 ingredients in a mixing bowl. In another bowl, whisk together remaining ingredients and add to wet mixture. Stir well until combined. Form into balls and chill or freeze.

Variations:
- Substitute half protein powder for coconut.
- Instead of Truvia, use 2 T. agave syrup or honey, and drop the tahini back to ½ cup plus 2 tablespoons so the mixture won't be too wet.
- Roll balls in sesame seeds, hemp seeds, coconut or crushed nuts.

Nutrition Facts

Serving Size (41g)
Servings Per Container

Amount Per Serving

Calories 180   Calories from Fat 130

	% Daily Value*
Total Fat 14g	**22%**
Saturated Fat 3.5g	**18%**
Trans Fat 0g	
Cholesterol 0mg	**0%**
Sodium 65mg	**3%**
Total Carbohydrate 15g	**5%**
Dietary Fiber 3g	**12%**
Sugars 6g	
Protein 4g	

Sugar-Free Lime–Tofu Pie

Makes 2 (9-inch) pies *Carol Nardello*

Here's a sugar-free version of lime pie, light and refreshing in hot weather, with tofu to add protein, nutrition and creamy texture.

2 (3-oz.)	packages of sugar-free lime-flavored Jell-O
2 c.	boiling water
14 oz.	soft tofu, drained
1 tsp.	lemon extract
1 T.	lemon juice
8 oz.	sugar-free whipped topping, thawed
2 (9-in.)	baked pie crusts

Mix Jell-O and boiling water together until completely dissolved. Chill until slightly thickened. In the bowl of a food processor, whip drained tofu until smooth. Add lemon extract and juice. Remove from processor and fold in whipped topping. Stir until smooth. Chill until gelatin has thickened and is slightly set. Mix with tofu mixture. Stir until well incorporated and streak-free. Pour into prepared pie crusts and chill several hours or until set. Serve cold.

Sugar-Free Pumpkin Pie

Makes 8 servings *Carol Nardello*

Is it possible to enjoy Thanksgiving without pumpkin pie? This recipe free of added sugar ensures that all your guests can indulge and enjoy a jazzed-up version containing fresh grated ginger. Intensely fragrant and delicious.

1 (15-oz.)	can mashed pumpkin
¾ c.	Splenda
½ tsp.	ginger, fresh-grated
1 tsp.	cinnamon
¼ tsp.	ground cloves
½ tsp.	salt
2	eggs, lightly beaten
1 (12-oz.)	can evaporated milk
1 (9-in.)	unbaked pie crust

Preheat oven to 425 degrees. Place pumpkin in a medium bowl and add Splenda, spices and salt, mixing well. Stir in eggs and milk and mix until smooth. Pour into pie crust and bake in hot oven for 15 minutes. Reduce heat to 350 degrees and continue baking for 45 minutes or until knife inserted in center comes out clean.

Nutrition Facts

Serving Size (144g)
Servings Per Container

Amount Per Serving

Calories 240 Calories from Fat 110

% Daily Value*

Total Fat 12g	18%
Saturated Fat 4.5g	23%
Trans Fat 0g	
Cholesterol 70mg	23%
Sodium 330mg	14%
Total Carbohydrate 24g	8%
Dietary Fiber 2g	8%
Sugars 6g	
Protein 6g	

No-Bake Pumpkin Pie

Makes 8 servings *Alyssa Moreau*

Here's another form of pumpkin pie, this one relying on ground nuts for texture and thickening. No need to worry about room in the oven at busy holiday time with this no-bake pie.

For the crust:
1¼ c.	pecans (skin-on or blanched)
¾ c.	pumpkin seeds
¼ tsp.	salt
1½ c.	chopped dates
1 tsp.	vanilla

For the filling:
1 c.	raw cashews
2 T.	agar flakes
⅛ tsp.	salt
1¼ c.	boiling water

1 (15-oz.)	can pumpkin
¼ c.	maple syrup
¼ c. + 2 T.	refined coconut oil
2 pckt.	Truvia
1 T.	vanilla
2-3 tsp.	cinnamon
¼ tsp.	nutmeg
¼ tsp.	cloves
1 tsp.	ginger
⅛ tsp.	allspice

For the crust: Pulse nuts, seeds and salt in a food processor until finely ground. Add chopped dates and vanilla; pulse again until incorporated. Pat into a lightly oiled pie 7-by-11-inch baking pan or dish.

For the filling: In a blender, process the cashews, agar flakes and salt until almost powdery. Add remaining ingredients and blend until smooth. Adjust flavor to taste; pour into prepared pie crust. Chill for at least 2 hours to set; preferably overnight.

Variations:
- Use other nuts (walnuts, almonds); 2 cups total.
- In place of Truvia, increase maple syrup to ½ cup; decrease boiling water to ¾ cup.
- Or to make the recipe sugar-free, use only Truvia (5 packets) and increase boiling water to 1½ cups.

Nutrition Facts

Serving Size (183g)
Servings Per Container

Amount Per Serving

Calories 440   Calories from Fat 250

% Daily Value*

Total Fat 28g	**43%**
Saturated Fat 6g	30%
Trans Fat 0g	
Cholesterol 0mg	**0%**
Sodium 120mg	**5%**
Total Carbohydrate 44g	**15%**
Dietary Fiber 7g	28%
Sugars 30g	
Protein 11g	

Okinawan Sweet Potato–Haupia Pie

Makes 8 servings   *Alyssa Moreau*

This is a new twist on a favorite combination of ingredients here in the Islands—coconut pudding and mashed Okinawan sweet potato. The haupia is uncooked, combining coconut creme and coconut oil to create a wonderful thick "haupia" layer on top of the sweet potato pie.

For the crust:

1 c.	whole wheat pastry flour
½ tsp.	baking powder
½ tsp.	cinnamon
⅛ tsp.	salt
2 T.	light oil
1 T	applesauce
1 T.	agave or honey
2-3 T.	water

For the haupia topping:

1 (15-oz.)	can light coconut milk
3 T.	cornstarch or arrowroot
2-4 T.	agave syrup
	Dash salt
½ in.	piece ginger, peeled, grated, pressed to extract juice
1 tsp.	coconut flakes, optional

For the filling:

2 c.	cooked Okinawan sweet potato, mashed
½ c.	almond milk (soy or rice milk can be substituted here)
3 T.	agave or honey
	Dash salt

Preheat oven to 350 degrees.

For the crust: Combine dry ingredients in a mixing bowl. Mix well. Separately, stir together the wet ingredients, then pour over the dry and combine until mixture forms a ball. Place on a flour-coated board and roll out into a circle. Place in an oiled 9-inch pie plate. Bake at 350 degrees for 10 minutes. Cool on rack.

For the filling: Combine sweet potato, almond milk, agave or honey and salt in a food processor and blend until smooth. If too thick, add a little water. Fill crust and smooth top. Bake at 350 degrees for 30 minutes. Cool on rack.

For the haupia topping: Combine coconut milk, cornstarch or arrowroot, salt and ginger in a medium sauce pan. Heat, stirring often until mixture comes to a boil. Reduce heat and then stir until thickened. Transfer to bowl and cool 10 minutes or longer then pour over the cooled pie. Sprinkle w/ coconut flakes. Chill for 2-4 hours to set

Nutrition Facts

Serving Size (90g)
Servings Per Container

Amount Per Serving

Calories 210   Calories from Fat 60

% Daily Value*

Total Fat 7g	**11%**
Saturated Fat 3g	**15%**
Trans Fat 0g	
Cholesterol 0mg	**0%**
Sodium 160mg	**7%**
Total Carbohydrate 35g	**12%**
Dietary Fiber 3g	**12%**
Sugars 16g	
Protein 2g	

Chocolate Pudding Pie

Makes 8 slices *Alyssa Moreau*

The creaminess and density of this dessert comes from ripe avocado, the sweetness from real maple syrup. You can also serve the filling in parfait glasses or a decorative bowl and garnish with berries or mint.

For the crust:
- ¾ c.   unsalted raw macadamia nuts
- ½ c.   dates, pitted and snipped into small pieces*
-         Dash salt

For the filling:
- 2 c.   ripe avocado
- ½ c.   dates, pitted and snipped into small pieces
- ½ c.   maple syrup
- 2 T.   refined coconut oil
- ½ tsp. vanilla
- ½ c.   cocoa, sifted if lumpy
- ⅛ tsp. salt

For the crust: Process the nuts in a food processor until they are a fine meal. Add the pitted dates and salt. Process until mixture sticks together. Transfer to a lightly oiled pie plate. (Use coconut or macadamia nut oil.)

For the filling: Combine all ingredients in a blender and blend until smooth. Pour into crust and, using a spatula, spread evenly. Chill several hours or overnight.

*Use kitchen shears to cut the dates instead of a knife; the task will be easier and less sticky. Dipping the shears in warm water between snips helps.

Nutrition Facts

Serving Size (99g)
Servings Per Container

Amount Per Serving

Calories 310   Calories from Fat 170

	% Daily Value*
Total Fat 19g	29%
Saturated Fat 6g	30%
Trans Fat 0g	
Cholesterol 0mg	0%
Sodium 80mg	3%
Total Carbohydrate 37g	12%
Dietary Fiber 7g	28%
Sugars 27g	
Protein 3g	

Baked Doughnuts

Makes 12 full-size doughnuts or 18 mini doughnuts *Alyssa Moreau*

Here's an idea for a special treat: baked doughnuts. Instead of being deep-fried, they're baked in a mold and made with higher-fiber whole wheat flour, Truvia in place of refined sugar, vegan egg replacer and a lowfat margarine. Doughnut molds can be found at stores that carry kitchen supplies as well as online. They come in full or mini sizes. If you purchase mini size, this recipe makes around 18.

For the doughnuts:
- ¾ c. whole wheat pastry flour
- ½ c. unbleached white flour
- 1½ tsp. baking powder
- 3 pckt. Truvia (optional)
- ½ tsp. salt
- ½ tsp. cinnamon
- ¼ tsp. nutmeg
- 1 T. Ener-G egg replacer
- 2 T. water
- ½ c. agave or maple syrup
- ½ c. almond or soymilk
- ½ tsp. cider or rice vinegar
- ¼ c. Earth Balance margarine, melted (or light oil)
- 1 tsp. vanilla

For the glaze:
- ⅓ c. almond or soy milk
- 2 T. maple syrup
- 1 tsp. arrowroot or cornstarch
- ½ tsp. vanilla
- Pinch salt

Garnish or sprinkle:
- 1 pckt. Truvia
- ⅛ tsp. cinnamon

Preheat oven to 350 degrees. Lightly coat doughnut mold with oil (spray or wipe with oiled paper towel).

To make doughnuts: Combine dry ingredients in a large mixing bowl. In a separate bowl, whisk together the egg replacer and water until dissolved and a bit frothy. Add remaining wet ingredients and stir well. Pour into the dry mixture and stir until combined. Fill each doughnut mold half full of batter. Bake 12-15 minutes or until a toothpick inserted in the doughnut comes out clean. Remove doughnuts and cool on rack.

To make the glaze: In a small saucepan, combine almond or soy milk, maple syrup, vanilla and salt and whisk in arrowroot or cornstarch, stirring to dissolve. Place over medium heat and stir until thickened. Drizzle over baked doughnuts.

To garnish: Combine Truvia and cinnamon and sprinkle over glaze.

Nutrition Facts

Serving Size (58g)
Servings Per Container

Amount Per Serving	
Calories 140	Calories from Fat 35
	% Daily Value*
Total Fat 4g	6%
Saturated Fat 1g	5%
Trans Fat 0g	
Cholesterol 0mg	0%
Sodium 220mg	9%
Total Carbohydrate 26g	9%
Dietary Fiber 1g	4%
Sugars 13g	
Protein 2g	

Coffee "Jell-O" with Coconut Whipped Creme

Makes 4 servings   *Alyssa Moreau*

Agar flakes, a form of kanten, are good for you as well as easy to work with. Here, just a drizzle of agave syrup sweetens an entire dessert. Alter the flavor by the type of coffee used—a stronger or mellower roast or even a flavored coffee.

2 c.	freshly brewed coffee
1 T.	agar flakes
2-4 T.	agave syrup, or to taste

In a small saucepan, whisk together the coffee and agar. Bring to a boil and cover. Reduce to a simmer and cook 10 minutes, whisking occasionally to help dissolve the agar flakes. Whisk in the agave and pour into a serving bowl or individual serving cups. Hold at room temperature a few hours or until firm. Cover and chill, if desired. Serve with a dollop of coconut creme (recipe follows).

Variation: Pour agar mixture into a flat dish. When gelled, cut into cube shapes. Roll cubes in kinako (toasted soybean powder).

Coconut Whipped Creme: Chill 1 can coconut milk (Thai Kitchen brand works well) overnight. Chill a medium bowl. Pierce bottom of can and drain out liquid (reserve for other uses). Open top of can and scoop out coconut creme and place in chilled mixing bowl. Whip with electric mixer until peaks form. Incorporate 2 tablespoons agave syrup (more or less, to taste). Chill 2 hours or until ready to serve.

Nutrition Facts

Serving Size (177g)
Servings Per Container

Amount Per Serving

Calories 140   Calories from Fat 50

                                                                    % Daily Value*

Total Fat 6g	9%
Saturated Fat 5g	25%
Trans Fat 0g	
Cholesterol 0mg	0%
Sodium 20mg	1%
Total Carbohydrate 23g	8%
Dietary Fiber 1g	4%
Sugars 22g	
Protein 1g	

Azuki Bean Mochi Cake

Cut into 24 pieces *Alyssa Moreau*

These azuki bean mochi cakes are sweetened with honey and agave. Use canned, whole beans, not the koshian or tsubushian paste. (You can boil or pressure-cook dried beans, but be warned, they take a loooooong time and must be fully cooked.)

2-4 T.	toasted sesame seeds (black, white or both)
1 (16-oz.)	box mochiko (sweet rice flour)
1 tsp.	baking powder
¼ tsp.	salt
1 (15-oz.)	can coconut milk
¾ c.	honey or agave
1¼ c.	water
1 tsp.	vanilla
1 (15-oz.)	can azuki beans, rinsed and drained

Lightly grease a 9-by-13-inch baking dish or pan (unrefined coconut oil works well for greasing). Sprinkle with sesame seeds to cover bottom. Preheat oven to 350 degrees. In a large bowl, whisk together dry ingredients. In a separate bowl, combine wet ingredients except beans and mix well. Add wet ingredients to dry and stir well. Add azuki beans and stir until smooth. Pour into baking dish and spread flat with spatula. Top with more sesame seeds. Bake 40 minutes or until top is browned and firm. Cool and chill.

Variations:

- To make a half recipe, use an 8-by-8-inch pan.
- Substitute 5 packets Truvia for honey; increase liquid by ¾ cup.

Nutrition Facts

Serving Size (78g)
Servings Per Container

Amount Per Serving

Calories 200	Calories from Fat 40

	% Daily Value*
Total Fat 4.5g	7%
Saturated Fat 3.5g	18%
Trans Fat 0g	
Cholesterol 0mg	0%
Sodium 50mg	2%
Total Carbohydrate 35g	12%
Dietary Fiber 2g	8%
Sugars 8g	
Protein 5g	

Macadamia Nut Shortbread Cookies

Makes about 24 cookies *Alyssa Moreau*

Ground nuts replace part of the flour in this butter-free shortbread, and agave or brown rice syrup takes the place of conventional sugar.

1 c.	whole wheat pastry flour
1 c.	unbleached white flour
1 c.	brown rice flour
1 tsp.	baking powder
½ tsp.	salt
½ c.	macadamia nuts, processed into meal
½ c.	light oil such as high-oleic safflower, grapeseed or canola
⅔ c.	agave or brown rice syrup
2 tsp.	vanilla
¼ c.	Garnish: macadamia pieces

Preheat oven to 350 degrees. In large mixing bowl, whisk together dry ingredients. In a small bowl, combine liquid ingredients. Pour liquids into dry ingredients and stir to combine. Sandwich dough between two pieces of waxed paper or kitchen parchment and roll to ¼ inch thick. Cut into 3-inch circles or squares. Arrange on parchment-lined cookie sheet; place a nut piece in the center of each cookie. Bake for 10-14 minutes (check at 10 minutes). Cool on rack.

Nutrition Facts

Serving Size (35g)
Servings Per Container

Amount Per Serving

Calories 160   Calories from Fat 70

% Daily Value*

Total Fat 8g	12%
Saturated Fat 1g	5%
Trans Fat 0g	
Cholesterol 0mg	0%
Sodium 70mg	3%
Total Carbohydrate 20g	7%
Dietary Fiber 1g	4%
Sugars 7g	
Protein 2g	

Sugar-Free Banana Snack Cake

Makes 12 pieces *Carol Nardello*

This recipe was developed to use up ripe bananas and to highlight the popular "banoffee" flavor that combines banana, coffee and cinnamon. The ripeness of the bananas determines how sweet the cake is. If bananas ripen before you are ready to bake, peel and place in zippered plastic bags in the freezer. They will keep for months. Defrost and mash as needed. Transfer any leftover mashed banana into a measuring cup. Fill to ¾ c. with milk. The extra bananas then can replace some of the milk in the recipe.

2 c.	flour
2 tsp.	baking powder
1 tsp.	baking soda
1 tsp.	instant coffee or espresso powder
1 tsp.	cinnamon
½ c.	Smart Balance margarine
¼ c.	Splenda
3	eggs, beaten
1 c.	mashed very ripe bananas
1 tsp.	vanilla
¾ c.	milk
1 c.	walnuts, chopped

Preheat oven to 350 degrees. Grease an 11-by-7-inch baking dish or pan. In a large mixing bowl, combine flour, baking powder, baking soda, instant coffee and cinnamon. In a medium bowl, cream together the margarine and Splenda until light. Stir in the eggs, bananas and vanilla until smooth. Add to flour mixture alternately with milk. Stir in nuts and pour into prepared pan. Bake in hot oven for 35-40 minutes or until toothpick inserted in center comes out clean.

Nutrition Facts

Serving Size (88g)
Servings Per Container

Amount Per Serving

Calories 230   Calories from Fat 120

	% Daily Value*
Total Fat 14g	22%
Saturated Fat 3g	15%
Trans Fat 0g	
Cholesterol 55mg	18%
Sodium 280mg	12%
Total Carbohydrate 23g	8%
Dietary Fiber 2g	8%
Sugars 4g	
Protein 6g	

CHAPTER FIVE

Egg 'Em On— with Egg Alternatives

Custard without eggs? Cakes with just one or two where three or four would normally be used? It can be done, and in most cases, diners won't taste the difference.

Alternatives to Eggs

Eggs—whether to eat them, how often to eat them, what to substitute—have long been a subject of debate among people concerned about their heart health (because of eggs' cholesterol content), as well as to vegetarians.

What do eggs do, and what can you use instead?

- Whole eggs: Used for leavening, emulsifying, tenderizing, flavoring and binding baked goods. One egg contains about 213 milligrams of dietary cholesterol. The daily recommended cholesterol limit is less than 300 milligrams for people with normal LDL (bad) cholesterol levels. Such people should eat eggs only if cholesterol from other sources—such as meats, poultry and dairy products—is limited (eggs OR bacon, but not both!). Remember to count eggs used as ingredients in baked goods and other preparations, not just eggs you eat separately. People with high LDL blood cholesterol levels or who are taking a blood cholesterol-lowering medication should eat less than 200 mg of cholesterol per day.

- Liquid egg substitutes: Made primarily of egg whites, refrigerated liquid egg substitutes such as Egg Beaters may produce dry baked goods and overfirm custards. However, if they're used in a 1-to-1 or 2-to-1 ratio with whole eggs, moisture and creaminess will be retained. Found near the eggs in most grocery stores and may be frozen for long keeping.

- Refrigerated egg-white products: These are found in the chill case in cartons (powdered) or jars (liquid). Powdered egg whites (e.g., Just Whites brand) are heat-pasteurized so cannot be used to make meringues or in applications where foamy egg whites are required. They are, however, the least expensive option. Liquid egg whites (e.g., Eggology) are more expensive but can be whipped. Either type is more effective than egg substitutes when a foamy batter is called for. Use them in a 1-to-1 ratio of whites to whole eggs. Found near the eggs in most grocery stores, and can be frozen.

- Powdered egg white: This product must be mixed with water (follow manufacturer directions). These work well in making meringues or when whipped egg whites are called for. As powdered egg white is pasteurized, it is particularly useful in uncooked recipes (no worries about salmonella or other food-borne illness). Powdered egg white is pretty expensive, but will last a long time in the pantry if kept away from moisture. Found in the baking section of some grocery stores, kitchen specialty stores and Whole Foods.

- Powdered vegan egg replacer: These products—Ener-G is our favorite and was used in testing many recipes in this book—are blended with water to approximate the texture of egg (follow manufacturer directions). Made from various natural starches, these work well in baking, but cannot replace egg whites in meringues and cannot be whipped. They store well if kept away from moisture. Baking section of natural food stores. Another option is whey protein powder (a cheese by-product): mix 1 tablespoon whey protein powder to 2 tablespoons water to equal 1 egg. Found in bodybuilding and nutrition stores.

- Other foods: When the primary function of the egg in a recipe is to add moisture, mashed banana or applesauce can be substituted; in this case, baking powder and soda do the leavening. Mashed tofu, with its texture similar to soft scrambled eggs, works well as an egg substitute in quiches, frittatas and scrambled egg-type dishes; other ingredients such as spices, condiments, aromatics and sauteed vegetables mask any tofu flavor. When a binder is needed, such as in a burger or fritter, use mashed potatoes, oatmeal, bread or cracker crumbs, tomato paste, Vegenaise or ketchup. Many vegetarians use ground flax seeds to replace eggs: 2 tablespoons ground flax seeds to 6 tablespoons hot water stands in for two eggs (let the flax seeds steep for 10 minutes before use).

- Or just skip it: When just 1 egg is called for, you can often get away with just eliminating it.

— Sharon Kobayashi

Eggless Oat Muffins

Makes 10-12 full-size muffins* Wanda Adams

Oat bran muffins became all the rage when research indicated that oats can help reduce "bad" cholesterol. In addition to containing oats, this recipe is made healthier still by the elimination of eggs, the reduction of sugar and the use of nonfat dairy products. To make the muffins dairy-free, use silken tofu instead of yogurt and apple or other juice instead of milk.

½ c.	water or apple juice	½ t.	baking soda
¼ c.	raisins, Craisins, finely chopped dried apples or other dried fruit	½ c.	plain nonfat yogurt
2 c.	oat bran (fine or medium grind)	½ c.	nonfat milk
2 T.	Splenda Brown Sugar (half brown sugar and half Splenda)	1 t.	vanilla
2 t.	cinnamon		Egg substitute equivalent to two eggs (if using Ener-G, 1 tablespoon Ener-G plus 4 tablespoons water whisked together just before it's placed in the batter)
	Pinch salt		
1 t.	baking powder		

Preheat oven to 400 degrees. Spray a muffin tin with nonstick spray or line with paper muffin cups. In a small bowl, combine apple juice or water and dried fruit; soak at least 15 minutes. In a large bowl, combine oat bran, brown sugar, cinnamon, salt, baking powder and baking soda and whisk together. Form a well in the center. In a small bowl or measuring cup, stir together yogurt and milk; add vanilla. Pour into well. Pour apple juice and dried fruit into well. Add egg substitute. Stir just to combine; don't overmix. Batter will be loose and somewhat thin. Spoon batter into muffin cups. If any cups are not filled, half-fill with water for easier clean-up.

Variations:

- For plain muffins, eliminate dried fruit.
- Match the flavor of the dried fruit to the juice (e.g., dried apricots with apricot nectar instead of apple juice).
- Pour half the batter into the cups, drop in 1 teaspoon of sugar-free preserves, cover with batter.

*10 if you almost fill the cups; 12 if half full; or 15 mini muffins. For full-size muffins, bake 15 minutes. For mini muffins, bake 12 minutes. Do not overbake; these should be golden, not browned.

Nutrition Facts

Serving Size (64g)
Servings Per Container

Amount Per Serving

Calories 90	Calories from Fat 15

% Daily Value*

Total Fat 1.5g	**2%**
Saturated Fat 0g	**0%**
Trans Fat 0g	
Cholesterol 0mg	**0%**
Sodium 135mg	**6%**
Total Carbohydrate 24g	**8%**
Dietary Fiber 4g	**16%**
Sugars 5g	
Protein 5g	

Peppermint–Chocolate Chip Cookies

Makes 18-20 cookies *Alyssa Moreau*

Perfect for the holidays, these cookies will make Santa smile—especially if he's watching his cholesterol.

1 c.	oat flour	3-4 T.	almond or other milk
1 c.	barley flour	⅓ c.	light oil
½ tsp	baking soda	⅓ c.	agave syrup
½ tsp.	baking powder	½ tsp.	vanilla extract
¼ tsp.	salt	½ tsp.	peppermint extract
1 T.	dry egg replacer (Ener-G)	¼ c.	chocolate chips

Preheat oven to 350 degrees. Line a baking sheet with parchment paper. Combine dry ingredients except egg replacer in a large mixing bowl. In another bowl, whisk the dry egg replacer together with the orange juice; it should thicken up. Add remaining wet ingredients. Blend wet into dry mixture and stir until just combined. Add chocolate chips. Drop by tablespoonfuls onto the baking sheet and bake for 10-12 minutes (check at 10 minutes) or until just browned. Cool on baking rack.

Variations:
- Use whole wheat pastry flour instead of oat and barley flour.
- Omit the peppermint and use orange extract instead.
- For gluten-free cookies, substitute equal amounts of brown rice/sorghum/tapioca flour and add ½ tsp. guar or xanthan gum.
- Substitute 3 T. of Just Like Sugar for agave syrup and increase the liquid to ⅓ cup.
- Make Kā'ū orange–peppermint–chocolate chip cookies by adding 2 teaspoons grated Kā'ū orange rind and orange juice for the milk. Use Just Like Sugar, which has a vaguely orange taste, in place of agave.

Nutrition Facts

Serving Size (28g)
Servings Per Container

Amount Per Serving	
Calories 130	Calories from Fat 45
	% Daily Value*
Total Fat 5g	8%
Saturated Fat 1g	5%
Trans Fat 0g	
Cholesterol 0mg	0%
Sodium 75mg	3%
Total Carbohydrate 17g	6%
Dietary Fiber 1g	4%
Sugars 6g	
Protein 2g	

Mini Vegetable Frittatas

Makes 6 servings *Sharon Kobayashi*

This fritatta is mostly vegetables, so egg substitute acts as a binder rather than a base. Use a good-quality, flavorful cheese to add richness. This is great alone as finger food, or you can also top the frittata with a dab of Greek yogurt or fat-free cream cheese and some chopped fresh tomato or a little smoked salmon or lean turkey or ham for a light meal. The frittata also makes a good filling for oat biscuits (p. 69): a less-fat version of those Mickey D's breakfast muffins. Silicon baking molds are great if you are watching fat since they do not require greasing. Never use cooking spray on silicon, as it will clog the micro-pores.

½ tsp.	oil
2 cloves	garlic, minced
12	cherry tomatoes, halved (or ½ large Roma tomato, chopped)
8 oz.	frozen spinach, chopped (or broccoli or Swiss chard)
¼ tsp.	fish sauce (or anchovy paste)
¼ tsp.	pepper
¼ tsp.	red pepper flakes, or to taste
1 T.	grated Parmesan cheese (or Pecorino Romano)
6 T.	egg substitute

Preheat oven to 325 degrees. Preheat a non-stick pan over medium-high heat, add oil and garlic and sauté briefly. Add tomatoes, spinach, fish sauce, pepper and red pepper. Cook till most of the liquid evaporates and tomatoes start to soften. Divide mixture into a 6-muffin silicon baking mold or non-stick muffin tin. Add ½ tsp. Parmesan and 1 T. egg substitute to each cup. Bake for 30 minutes or till egg is firm, but not browned. There may be a little liquid on top; it will settle as it cools. Cool completely in pan before removing to plate.

Nutrition Facts

Serving Size (91g)
Servings Per Container

Amount Per Serving

Calories 40   Calories from Fat 15

	% Daily Value*
Total Fat 1.5g	2%
Saturated Fat 0g	0%
Trans Fat 0g	
Cholesterol 0mg	0%
Sodium 120mg	5%
Total Carbohydrate 3g	1%
Dietary Fiber 1g	4%
Sugars 1g	
Protein 3g	

No-Egg Salad

Makes 4-6 servings *Wanda Adams*

If egg salad sandwiches are a favorite, try this. If you're afraid of too much tofu flavor, ease change by using 1 hard-boiled egg for every ¼ cup tofu.

1 block	silken tofu, drained
3 T.	minced flat-leaf parsley
2 T.	finely minced onion
½	stalk celery, finely minced
½ c.	conventional or lowfat mayonnaise or Vegenaise
1 T.	mustard (yellow, Dijon or stoneground coarse style)
1 tsp.	fresh lemon juice
	Lots of fresh-ground black pepper

In a bowl, combine all ingredients. Taste and correct seasonings. Serve on whole-grain bread, fill pita halves or spread on bagel crisps or crackers.

Variations:
- Add to taste: chopped, seeded olives; pickle relish; chopped pimentos; herbs such as dill or tarragon; spices such as paprika, curry or cayenne; chopped shallots or horseradish; chopped vegetables such as tomato, cucumber, carrot or jicama; shredded cheese.
- If you're not a vegan, hard-boil a dozen eggs; cool, peel and halve them. Discard the yolks and fill the halved whites with No-Egg Salad.

Nutrition Facts

Serving Size (162g)
Servings Per Container

Amount Per Serving

Calories 240   Calories from Fat 180

	% Daily Value*
Total Fat 21g	32%
Saturated Fat 3g	15%
Trans Fat 0g	
Cholesterol 0mg	0%
Sodium 230mg	10%
Total Carbohydrate 5g	2%
Dietary Fiber 1g	4%
Sugars 0g	
Protein 5g	

Eggnog Pudding

Makes 6 servings *Sharon Kobayashi*

Eggnog is an old recipe—milk, egg yolks, nutmeg and brandy. To cut the cholesterol and fat, this recipe substitutes garbanzo beans, which have an egg-like flavor, for some of the egg. Evaporated milk adds richness usually supplied by half-and-half or heavy cream. Pudding should have a smooth texture, so it is very important to strain the mixture before cooling to remove pieces of bean, nutmeg or eggshell. Freshly grated nutmeg is essential to this recipe. If you don't have a nutmeg grater, use a fine cheese grater. Whole nutmeg is grown locally by Wailea Ag Group on the Big Island, and can sometimes be found at the Saturday Market at Kapi'olani Community College. Nutmeg is also widely available in the spice section of grocery stores and Indian or Asian markets.

⅓ c.	canned garbanzo beans, rinsed and drained (salt-free or 90-percent reduced salt)
1⅓ c.	lowfat milk, divided
1 c.	fat-free evaporated milk
½ tsp.	freshly grated nutmeg
¼ tsp.	turmeric, ground
2 T.	cornstarch
3 T.	sugar
1 T.	brandy
1 tsp.	vanilla extract
1 lg.	egg
1 T.	unsalted butter

Optional garnish: Top each portion with 1 tsp fat-free whipped topping and light dusting of nutmeg or cinnamon

In a blender, purée beans with ⅓ c. of the milk until smooth. In a heavy-bottomed pot, combine bean mixture, remaining milk and evaporated milk. Add nutmeg and turmeric; cook on medium-high until mixture boils, stirring occasionally. In a heat-safe bowl, whisk together cornstarch, sugar, brandy, vanilla and egg until smooth. Pour boiling milk over egg mixture while whisking constantly. Pudding should thicken immediately. Use a silicon spatula to push pudding through a fine sieve. Whisk in butter; place piece of plastic wrap directly over pudding. Refrigerate until completely cool.

Nutrition Facts

Serving Size (135g)
Servings Per Container

Amount Per Serving

Calories 140   Calories from Fat 30

% Daily Value*

Total Fat 3.5g	5%
Saturated Fat 2g	10%
Trans Fat 0g	
Cholesterol 45mg	15%
Sodium 95mg	4%
Total Carbohydrate 20g	7%
Dietary Fiber 1g	4%
Sugars 15g	
Protein 6g	

Raspberries and Cream French Toast

Makes 1 dozen sandwiches   *Carol Nardello*

How about baked French toast filled with raspberries and cream for a late-night snack? Using fat-free and lowfat products makes this one healthier.

For the French toast:

1 (1-lb.)	loaf soft French bread about 18 inches long
4 oz.	⅓-less-fat cream cheese, softened
½ c.	sugar-free raspberry preserves
1 c.	fat-free egg substitute (e.g., Egg Beaters)
1 c.	skim milk
1 T.	Splenda
1 T.	cinnamon
¼ tsp.	salt

For the raspberry sauce:

10-oz.	bag frozen whole raspberries, thawed
¼ c.	Splenda
1 T.	lemon juice
2 tsp.	cornstarch

Grease or oil-spray a 9-by-13-inch baking pan. Slice bread into 24 (¾-inch-thick) pieces. Spread half the bread slices with reduced-fat cheese and the other half with preserves. Press together to form sandwiches and arrange into prepared pan. In a medium bowl, whip egg substitute, milk, Splenda, cinnamon and salt together. Pour over sandwiches. Allow them to rest 5 minutes until liquid is absorbed. Preheat oven to 400 degrees. Cover dish with foil and bake in hot oven for 15 minutes. Remove foil and continue baking for 20 minutes longer or until golden brown. In a small saucepan, combine sauce ingredients and bring to a boil. Stirring frequently, boil 1 minute or until thickened. Remove from heat and strain out seeds. Pour into small pitcher. Serve warm with French toast.

Variations:

Substitute blueberry or blackberry jam and frozen blueberries. Or use mango or mango-pineapple jam and fresh or frozen mango.

Nutrition Facts

Serving Size (127g)
Servings Per Container

Amount Per Serving

Calories 300   Calories from Fat 25

	% Daily Value*
Total Fat 3g	5%
Saturated Fat 1g	5%
Trans Fat 0g	
Cholesterol 5mg	2%
Sodium 690mg	29%
Total Carbohydrate 57g	19%
Dietary Fiber 2g	8%
Sugars 4g	
Protein 13g	

Eggless Cup Custards

Makes 6 servings *Wanda Adams*

Islanders love, love, love custard, especially in pie. Here's an alternative to such fat-laden dishes.

2½ c.	nonfat evaporated milk or soy milk
1	vanilla bean (preferably Hawaiian)
¾ c.	Splenda (or sugar, if you prefer)
¼ tsp.	salt
⅛ tsp.	ground nutmeg
3 tsp.	Ener-G vegan egg replacer

Preheat oven to 350 degrees. Boil enough water to half-fill a 9-by-13-inch baking dish or pan. Have ready 6 heatproof ramekins or heatproof custard cups, set in the pan; ramekins should not touch. Place milk or soy milk in a medium saucepan over medium-high heat. Split vanilla bean and scrape the seeds into the milk. Throw in the bean. Allow bean to steep as milk heats to scalding (small bubbles appear around perimeter). In a medium mixing bowl, whisk together Splenda, salt and nutmeg. Remove vanilla bean from hot milk and gradually strain hot vanilla-flavored milk through fine-mesh strainer into bowl with Splenda and flavorings. Mix Ener-G with 3 tablespoons hot water, whisking well to combine. Whisk egg replacer into milk mixture. Pour milk–egg mixture into ramekins in even portions. Carefully pour hot water into 9-by-13 pan until water comes three-quarters of the way up the sides of the ramekins. Place in oven. Bake 30-45 minutes until nearly set, still slightly soft but not totally liquid. Cool. Serve at room temperature or chilled.

Variations:

- Chocolate custard: Omit vanilla bean. Whisk ¼ cup unsweetened Dutch-process cocoa into a small amount of the hot milk until smooth and incorporated; add to milk. Proceed with recipe. A few shaved curls of dark semisweet chocolate may be used for garnish.
- Coconut custard: Instead of evaporated or soy milk, use fat-reduced coconut milk. Omit vanilla beans and nutmeg. Sprinkle the bottom of each ramekin with a teaspoon of finely shredded unsweetened coconut—fresh or dried (health food store). Proceed with recipe. Toast ½ cup fresh or dried coconut in a metal baking pan until golden and fragrant (do this the same time you're baking the custard). Use this to garnish the finished custards.

Nutrition Facts

Serving Size (58g)
Servings Per Container

Amount Per Serving	
Calories 60	Calories from Fat 0

	% Daily Value*
Total Fat 0g	0%
Saturated Fat 0g	0%
Trans Fat 0g	
Cholesterol 0mg	0%
Sodium 115mg	5%
Total Carbohydrate 10g	3%
Dietary Fiber 0g	0%
Sugars 7g	
Protein 3g	

CHAPTER SIX

The Staff of Life: Baking Healthful Bread

In the era of low-carbohydrate diets, bread became The Enemy. But bread recipes that don't rely on fat and sweeteners and make use of higher-fiber whole grains are both satisfying—giving a feeling of fullness—and more healthful. We've collected a variety of breads, rolls, muffins, even pizza, that embody these ideas.

Alternatives to All-Purpose Flour

Unless there is someone with gluten intolerance in the house, it's likely that the only flour you stock is all-purpose flour (10-12 percent protein). If you bake a great deal, you may stock high-protein bread flour (12-14 percent protein; the springy gluten traps gasses and lightens bread), whole wheat flour (12-15 percent protein; higher fiber and more nutritional value) and perhaps cake flour. Many people prefer unbleached all-purpose flour, which is higher in protein and has not been chemically treated. Lower-gluten all-purpose or pastry flours (5-8 percent protein), such as the South's coveted White Lily brand, are made from soft red winter wheat and are favored for biscuits and other pastry. Cake flour (6-8 percent protein) is best for cakes, quick breads and biscuits; to substitute cake flour for all-purpose flour use 1 cup plus 2 tablespoons cake flour for every cup of all-purpose flour.

Two others worth considering, and increasingly available, are:

- White whole wheat flour: Ground from a different strain of wheat, this flour appears white but has more fiber than all-purpose flour. Natural foods stores and some groceries.
- Whole wheat pastry flour: This flour is lighter and finer textured than all-purpose flour but higher in fiber and nutrients. It can be used in cookies, cakes, breads, pastries—wherever all-purpose flour is called for. Health food stores.

Because of their higher oil content, whole wheat flours pick up flavors and go rancid more rapidly than cake or all-purpose flours. Store them in an airtight container in the freezer if you're keeping them longer than a week or two. Whole wheat pastry flour can be purchased in bulk in health food stores in small quantities.

Honey Whole Wheat Dough

Makes 6 ounces of dough* *Sharon Kobayashi*

Whole wheat flour has less gluten than the high-protein white flour commonly used for pizza dough. White whole wheat flour is ground from a different variety of wheat, with a mild wheat flavor, so is more versatile. White whole wheat is widely available at supermarkets. This dough can be used to make savory pizza as well as sweet.

1 tsp.	rapid-rise yeast
¼ c.	warm water
½ tsp.	sugar
¾ c.	white whole wheat flour
	(substitute ½ c. whole wheat plus ¼ c. white flour)
¼ tsp.	salt
¼ tsp.	cinnamon
1 T.	extra light olive oil
1 T.	honey

In a mixing bowl, sprinkle yeast over warm water, add sugar and let "proof" 5 minutes. When yeast is frothy, add flour to cover. Add remaining ingredients and, using your hands, mix to combine. Dough should be soft but not sticky. Add a little extra flour if dough is too wet. Knead briefly and cover with a light kitchen towel. Let dough rest 1 hour, or until doubled in volume.

Note: This versatile recipe is used in other preparations in this book; it's a building block you can use in many ways.

*Use for pizza or 1 small loaf of bread.

Nutrition Facts

Serving Size (232g)
Servings Per Container

Amount Per Serving

Calories 290	Calories from Fat 70

	% Daily Value*
Total Fat 8g	12%
Saturated Fat 1g	5%
Trans Fat 0g	
Cholesterol 0mg	0%
Sodium 300mg	13%
Total Carbohydrate 46g	15%
Dietary Fiber 7g	28%
Sugars 9g	
Protein 7g	

Strawberry–Ricotta Pizza

Makes 6 servings   *Sharon Kobayashi*

This is an elegant, easy dessert. If you like, substitute raspberries, plums or poha and use a complementary jam flavor. The jam adds sweetness and heightens the fruit flavor. For best results, scatter a little cornmeal on the bottom of the pan or pizza peel to prevent sticking. If you have a pizza stone, place it in the oven while preheating. If you don't have one, during the last 5 minutes of baking, place the pizza directly on the oven rack to crisp the bottom. It is important to brush the crust with the egg white and set it by cooking it slightly, as this provides a moisture barrier and prevents a soggy crust.

	Honey Whole Wheat dough (previous recipe)
1	egg white, beaten slightly
6 lg.	strawberries, roughly chopped (may use frozen)
2 T.	strawberry jam
6 T.	part-skim ricotta cheese
2 tsp.	sugar
¼ tsp.	lemon zest (½ lemon)
½ tsp.	cornstarch
	Berries and mint sprigs for garnish

Prepare dough as directed; preheat oven to 450 degrees. Combine strawberries and jam in a food processor. Pulse till puréed, but leave some texture (you should get about ½ c.). Roll out dough to 10 inches in diameter. Brush dough with half of the egg white. Combine remaining white with cheese, sugar and zest. Place crust in oven for 2-3 minutes, or until egg white sets. Remove crust from oven and spread strawberry mixture evenly over dough. Place 8 (1-T.) dollops of ricotta mixture at even intervals on top. Bake for 12-15 minutes or until crust is golden brown. Cool slightly on a cooling rack before serving, or serve at room temperature.

Nutrition Facts

Serving Size (145g)
Servings Per Container

Amount Per Serving

Calories 150   Calories from Fat 25

% Daily Value*

Total Fat 2.5g	4%
Saturated Fat 0g	0%
Trans Fat 0g	
Cholesterol 5mg	2%
Sodium 160mg	7%
Total Carbohydrate 24g	8%
Dietary Fiber 3g	12%
Sugars 10g	
Protein 6g	

Whole Wheat Rolls

Makes 8 servings *Sharon Kobayashi*

This is another building block recipe. White flour and a little sugar together with the whole wheat make this recipe very flexible and amenable to a variety of fillings and/or toppings. Instead of rolls, you can use a loaf pan to make bread for sandwiches or flatten the dough to make pita bread or manapua (such as the "Near East Manapua" recipe, which follows).

1 c.	water
1 tsp.	rapid-rise yeast
2 T.	sugar
½ tsp.	salt
1 T.	canola oil
1¼ c.	whole wheat flour
¾ c.	all-purpose flour

Combine water, yeast and sugar in a mixing bowl. Let "proof" 5 minutes, or until mixture begins to foam. Add remaining ingredients and mix well to combine. Turn out onto a floured board and knead briefly. Return to mixing bowl, cover and let rise 1 hour or until doubled in size. Turn out to a floured board and cut into 8 pieces. Roll each piece into a ball. Line a baking sheet with parchment paper or a silicon sheet. Preheat oven to 400. Place dough balls (evenly spaced) on the baking sheet. Spray lightly with water and let rise 45 minutes, or till doubled in size. Bake for 20 minutes or until brown. Transfer rolls to a wire rack to cool.

Nutrition Facts

Serving Size (63g)
Servings Per Container

Amount Per Serving

Calories 120 Calories from Fat 10

% Daily Value*

Total Fat 1g	2%
Saturated Fat 0g	0%
Trans Fat 0g	
Cholesterol 0mg	0%
Sodium 150mg	6%
Total Carbohydrate 24g	8%
Dietary Fiber 3g	12%
Sugars 3g	
Protein 4g	

Herb Braided Bread

Makes 1 loaf *Carol Nardello*

This more healthful and brightly flavored version of Jewish challah makes use of a sugar substitute and reduced-fat milk and margarine to cut fat while employing herbs to add flavor interest. Be sure to use fresh herbs.

1	clove garlic, minced	1½ tsp.	salt
2 T.	fresh rosemary, chopped and divided	¾ c.	nonfat milk
		½ c.	water
1 T.	fresh thyme, chopped	¼ c.	Smart Balance margarine
1 T.	fresh oregano, chopped	1	egg, beaten
1 T.	fresh basil, chopped	1 T.	Smart Balance margarine, melted
4¼ c	all-purpose flour		
1½ T.	Splenda		Dash coarse sea salt
2 (¼-oz.)	pkg. rapid-rise instant yeast		

On a cutting board, mince garlic and very finely chop 1 T. rosemary with remaining fresh herbs. Reserve the second tablespoon of rosemary for garnish. In a large bowl, combine 1½ c. flour, Splenda, yeast, salt and chopped fresh herbs. In a saucepan over medium heat, warm the milk, water and ¼ c. margarine to 120-130 degrees or until margarine just begins to melt. Stir into yeast mixture until smooth. Add egg and enough of the remaining flour to form soft dough. Knead dough on a lightly floured surface for about 5 minutes or until smooth and elastic. Cover and rest on floured surface for 10 minutes.

Divide dough into 3 equal pieces. Roll each piece into a 30-inch rope. Braid the ropes together while tucking the ends underneath. Place on a lightly greased baking sheet. Cover and let rise in a warm, draft-free spot until doubled in size (about 20-40 minutes). Preheat oven to 375 degrees. Bake for 30 minutes. Melt 1 T. margarine and brush over baked bread. Chop 1 T. rosemary and sprinkle over bread. Sprinkle a dash of coarse sea salt on top and place on rack to cool.

Nutrition Facts

Serving Size (122g)
Servings Per Container

Amount Per Serving

Calories 300   Calories from Fat 70

% Daily Value*

Total Fat 8g	**12%**
Saturated Fat 1.5g	8%
Trans Fat 1.5g	
Cholesterol 30mg	**10%**
Sodium 560mg	**23%**
Total Carbohydrate 49g	**16%**
Dietary Fiber 2g	8%
Sugars 3g	
Protein 9g	

Near East Manapua

Make 8 servings   *Sharon Kobayashi*

The Moroccan-inspired, sweet–savory filling is different enough to be interesting, yet familiar enough to appeal to kids. Tofu keeps the filling moist, and the complex flavors are rich enough to keep the meat to a minimum. This is a substantial snack, and with fruit and veggie sticks is a good lunch. Freeze leftovers and reheat in a toaster oven.

½ c.	lean hamburger (packed) or 4 oz. ground lean lamb or turkey	7 oz.	soft tofu (about half a block)
½	onion, diced small	2 T.	ketchup
¼ tsp.	allspice	1 tsp.	red wine vinegar
¼ tsp.	pumpkin pie spice	½ tsp.	salt
2 T.	tomato paste	½ c.	low-sodium chicken broth
1 T.	flour	2 T.	pine nuts
2 T.	raisins—or white raisins, currants, dried apricots or plums, diced small	1 lb.	whole wheat rolls (previous recipe)

In a heavy-bottomed, non-stick pan, sauté hamburger and onion till brown. Add spices; sauté briefly. Add tomato paste and flour, stirring until incorporated. Add raisins, tofu, ketchup, vinegar, salt and broth. Cook until reduced to about 1½ c. Add pine nuts and continue to cook, stirring frequently. Mixture should brown deeply (like corned beef hash). Remove from heat when mixture is reduced to about 1 c. Cool and form 8 balls of filling mixture, about 2 T. each. Prepare whole wheat rolls (p. 61) as directed (up until making dough balls). Preheat oven to 400 degrees. With floured hands, flatten one dough ball slightly, and place 1 portion filling on top. Push filling down while pulling dough up and over (like stuffing a pillow case). Seal edges well, and set down on baking sheet, seam side down. Spray lightly with water; let rise 45 minutes or until doubled in size. Bake for 20-25 minutes or until brown. Cool on a wire rack before eating or freezing.

Nutrition Facts

Serving Size (135g)
Servings Per Container

Amount Per Serving

Calories 180   Calories from Fat 40

% Daily Value*

Total Fat 4g	**6%**
Saturated Fat 0.5g	3%
Trans Fat 0g	
Cholesterol 10mg	**3%**
Sodium 400mg	**17%**
Total Carbohydrate 28g	**9%**
Dietary Fiber 3g	12%
Sugars 6g	
Protein 10g	

Polenta Rolls

Make 8 servings *Sharon Kobayashi*

Partially cooked polenta makes this a soft roll, but with a little texture. Polenta is coarsely ground cornmeal and a good introduction to whole grains. This recipe is very easy for the first-time bread maker, and does not require kneading. The dough can be mixed and refrigerated overnight for the first rise, cutting down on prep time. If the dough does not rise the first time, try adding another teaspoon of yeast from a fresh packet (your yeast may be too old).

1½ c.	water
½ c.	polenta
1 tsp.	rapid rise yeast
1	egg
1 T.	olive oil
1 c.	all-purpose flour
½ tsp.	salt

Bring water to a boil, drizzle in polenta and reduce heat to a simmer. Cook, stirring frequently, for 7-8 minutes; remove from heat and transfer to a bowl. Cool for 15 minutes or until just warm. Add yeast, egg, oil, flour and salt. Mix well, cover and let rest 45 minutes to an hour (until doubled in volume). Preheat oven to 425 degrees. Spray a muffin tin with cooking spray (or use a silicon muffin pan). Dough will be soft. Mix a little to deflate slightly. Use a small ice cream scoop or 2 large spoons (like dropping cookie dough) to scoop dough into 8 muffin cups; let rise 30 minutes or till doubled in size. Bake for 25 minutes or till golden brown. Remove rolls from pan and cool on a rack. Freeze leftovers.

Nutrition Facts

Serving Size (77g)
Servings Per Container

Amount Per Serving

Calories 110   Calories from Fat 20

% Daily Value*

Total Fat 2.5g	4%
Saturated Fat 0g	0%
Trans Fat 0g	
Cholesterol 25mg	8%
Sodium 160mg	7%
Total Carbohydrate 18g	6%
Dietary Fiber 1g	4%
Sugars 0g	
Protein 3g	

Quick Apple–Date Sticky Buns

Make 8 servings *Sharon Kobayashi*

This dish—a whisked-together bread dough with fruit briefly pulsed and a bit of vanilla and maple syrup—is a great alternative to time-consuming traditional sticky buns. The flavor is reminiscent of candied apples. Drizzled over the jelly-rolled buns, the maple syrup caramelizes beautifully, and the flavor complements the filling and the toasty whole wheat. If, after inverting the buns when baked, you want them more deeply caramelized, run them under the broiler or flip them back into a cast-iron skillet and toast them on the stove on medium heat until the desired color is achieved.

1⅓ c.	whole wheat flour	6	medjool dates, seeded, roughly chopped
⅔ c.	oat flour		
½ T.	baking soda	1	Fuji or other crisp sweet apple, peeled, cored, roughly chopped
1 tsp.	baking powder		
½ T.	salt	1 tsp.	cinnamon
1 T.	canola oil	2 T.	unsalted butter, softened
¼ c.	part-skim ricotta cheese	1 T.	vanilla extract
¾ c.	buttermilk	¼ c.	pure maple syrup

Preheat oven to 400 degrees. In a mixing bowl, combine flours, baking soda, baking powder and salt. Whisk together. Add oil, ricotta and buttermilk. Mix well (it will be a little sticky) and cover. In a food processor, combine dates, apple and cinnamon. Pulse to roughly mince; reserve. Lay out a piece of plastic wrap, about 12 inches by 16 inches, and spray with cooking spray. Transfer dough to plastic, roughly shape into a square. Cover with another piece of wrap and roll out to 9 or 10 inches square. Uncover dough; spread apple mixture over square, leaving a half-inch margin on the side nearest you, and a 1-inch margin at the far edge. Use the plastic wrap as a guide to roll over (like a jelly roll) towards the 1-inch margin edge. Use a serrated knife with a gentle sawing motion to cut crosswise into 8 pieces. Spread butter on the bottom of an 8-inch round pan; a cast-iron skillet is perfect for this. Use a little of the butter to also grease the sides of the pan. Drizzle vanilla and syrup over rolls and place them, presentation-side-down, evenly spaced in pan. Place in oven and bake 30 minutes, until lightly browned and syrup thickens. Cool before eating.

Nutrition Facts

Serving Size (124g)
Servings Per Container

Amount Per Serving

Calories 290   Calories from Fat 60

% Daily Value*

Total Fat 6g	**9%**
Saturated Fat 2.5g	**13%**
Trans Fat 0g	
Cholesterol 10mg	**3%**
Sodium 330mg	**14%**
Total Carbohydrate 49g	**16%**
Dietary Fiber 6g	**24%**
Sugars 22g	
Protein 5g	

Banana–Mango–Macadamia Nut Muffins

Makes 10-12 muffins   *Alyssa Moreau*

These are wonderful muffins that are satisfying and hearty. If mangoes are not in season, you can add more banana to the blender mix.

1½ c.	whole wheat pastry flour
1 tsp.	baking powder
½ tsp.	salt
5 pckt.	Truvia
1 c.	boiling water
½ tsp.	baking soda
½ c.	dates
1 c.	mashed ripe banana
3 T.	oil
1 T.	dry egg replacer (such as Ener-G)
1 tsp.	vanilla
1 tsp.	light vinegar
½ c.	chopped fresh mango
½ c.	chopped macadamia nuts

Preheat oven to 350 degrees. Spray muffin pans with vegetable oil spray or line with silicon cups. Combine dry ingredients, not including egg replacer, in a medium mixing bowl. Boil water and place in blender with remaining liquid ingredients (including banana) and egg replacer. Blend until smooth. Add to the dry mixture and stir until just combined. Mix in the mango and macadamia nuts. Spoon batter into prepared muffin cups and bake 17-20 minutes or until a toothpick inserted comes out clean.

Variations:

- For a gluten-free version, substitute ½ c. each brown rice, sorghum and tapioca flours plus 1 tsp. guar or xanthan gum.
- Instead of Truvia, add ½ cup agave or honey to liquid ingredients and decrease boiling water to ⅔ cup.

Nutrition Facts

Serving Size (70g)
Servings Per Container

Amount Per Serving

Calories 150	Calories from Fat 70
	% Daily Value*
Total Fat 8g	12%
Saturated Fat 1g	5%
Trans Fat 0g	
Cholesterol 0mg	0%
Sodium 100mg	4%
Total Carbohydrate 21g	7%
Dietary Fiber 3g	12%
Sugars 8g	
Protein 3g	

Oat Biscuits

Makes 7 (1.5-oz.) servings *Sharon Kobayashi*

Blending oat flour with white whole wheat produces a light and mild flavor while delivering a good dose of whole grain. Using both butter and ricotta cheese gives this biscuit butter flavor and tenderness, with minimum fat. A bit of egg white helps to lighten the dough, because oat flour does not rise well. This is a versatile recipe, a good base for both sweet and savory—yet another building block. Because of the fat in the recipe, use "skinny" fillings, such as fruit or vegetables. Try it in the Strawberry Shortcake recipe (below) for dessert, as a snack sandwich with mini vegetable fritatta (p. 50), or hot out of the oven with vegetable soup for dinner. Leftovers freeze well. Reheat at 350 for 5 minutes.

1 c.	oat flour
½ c.	white whole wheat flour (or all-purpose)
1 T.	sugar
1 tsp.	baking powder
¼ tsp.	baking soda
¼ tsp.	salt
2 T.	unsalted butter
¼ c.	part-skim ricotta cheese
3 T.	egg substitute
¼ c.	buttermilk, plus extra for brushing top

Preheat oven to 400 degrees. In a medium bowl, whisk together dry ingredients. Cut in butter. Add cheese, egg and buttermilk, mix. Turn dough out onto a piece of plastic wrap. Flatten slightly; cover with another piece of plastic. Flatten out or roll to ½-inch thickness. Use 2¼-inch round cutter (or ⅓ c. measuring cup). Cut into 7 pieces, flouring cutter between uses. Transfer to parchment-lined or sprayed baking sheet. Brush tops with a little buttermilk. Bake for 15-20 minutes or till light brown.

Variations:
• To make oat biscuit strawberry shortcake: Mix 1 c. sliced strawberries with 4 tsp. agave syrup; chill 30 minutes, until juices run out. Split four oat biscuits, reserving the tops; scatter half the berries over the bottoms. Place 1 T. fat-free whipped topping on each berry-covered biscuit and add biscuit tops (like a sandwich). Top with remaining berries and 1 T. each whipped topping. Drizzle with berry juices. Or use mango or any smooth-textured tropical fruit, or peaches, nectarines or plums in season. Makes 4 servings.

Nutrition Facts

Serving Size (57g)
Servings Per Container

Amount Per Serving

Calories 190   Calories from Fat 50

	% Daily Value*
Total Fat 5g	8%
Saturated Fat 3g	15%
Trans Fat 0g	
Cholesterol 10mg	3%
Sodium 240mg	10%
Total Carbohydrate 23g	8%
Dietary Fiber 3g	12%
Sugars 2g	
Protein 5g	

Quick Morning Glory Muffins

Makes 12 muffins *Carol Nardello*

No sugar or fat is added to this easy fruit and nut muffin recipe.

1¼ c.	all-purpose or whole wheat pastry flour
1 tsp.	cinnamon
1 tsp.	baking soda
1 tsp.	baking powder
¼ tsp.	salt
1 sml.	apple, peeled and grated
½ c.	raisins
½ c.	dates, seeded and chopped
½ c.	dried cranberries
1	carrot, peeled and grated
2	eggs, beaten
½ c.	unsweetened applesauce
1 c.	water
1 tsp.	vanilla
½ c.	unsweetened shredded coconut (fresh or dried)

Preheat oven to 375 degrees. Grease or line a 12-cup muffin pan with paper liners.
In a large bowl, combine flour, cinnamon, baking soda, baking powder and salt. In a smaller bowl, combine fruits and carrot. In a third bowl, combine eggs, applesauce, water and vanilla.
Stir egg mixture into dry ingredients just until combined. Add mixed fruits and coconut and stir just until moistened. Avoid overmixing. Fill prepared muffin cups ⅔ full. Bake in hot oven for 25-30 minutes or until toothpick inserted in center comes out clean.

Nutrition Facts

Serving Size (89g)
Servings Per Container

Amount Per Serving

Calories 150	Calories from Fat 30

	% Daily Value*
Total Fat 3g	5%
Saturated Fat 2.5g	13%
Trans Fat 0g	
Cholesterol 35mg	12%
Sodium 220mg	9%
Total Carbohydrate 28g	9%
Dietary Fiber 2g	8%
Sugars 16g	
Protein 3g	

Sesame Biscuits

Makes 12 biscuits *Alyssa Moreau*

Try these biscuits in the morning warm with some local honey and your favorite tea. They also pair well with savory soups or stews. And they make a nice snack as is, when you're craving carbs between meals.

2 c.	whole wheat pastry flour
½ tsp.	salt
2 tsp.	baking powder
½ tsp.	baking soda
3 T.	light oil (light sesame is nice here)
2 T.	tahini
1 tsp.	vinegar (apple cider or rice)
¼ c. + 2 T.	warm water
1 T.	sesame seeds

Preheat oven to 375 degrees. In a large mixing bowl, whisk together dry ingredients (except sesame seeds). In a second bowl, whisk together wet ingredients; stir into dry ingredients to form a soft dough. Knead a few times. Lightly roll out on a floured board to form a round or rectangle ½ inch thick (don't overwork dough). Sprinkle with sesame seeds. Cut with 2-inch biscuit cutter or slice into squares or diamond shapes. Bake on a parchment-lined baking sheet 10 minutes or until nicely browned on top.

Nutrition Facts

Serving Size (36g)
Servings Per Container

Amount Per Serving

Calories 130 Calories from Fat 50

% Daily Value*

Total Fat 5g	8%
Saturated Fat 0.5g	3%
Trans Fat 0g	
Cholesterol 0mg	0%
Sodium 240mg	10%
Total Carbohydrate 17g	6%
Dietary Fiber 3g	12%
Sugars 0g	
Protein 3g	

Orange Yogurt Scones

Makes 8 scones *Alyssa Moreau*

"Skahns" they call them in Great Britain, and they're a must for high tea. Serve these citrusy, light-textured scones as an afternoon snack or at breakfast.

2 c.	whole wheat pastry flour
4 pckt.	Truvia (reserve one for topping)
1 tsp.	baking powder
¼ tsp.	baking soda
¼ tsp.	salt
3 T.	non-hydrogenated margarine (Earth Balance)
1 (6-oz.)	carton orange yogurt
1 T.	dry egg replacer mixed w/ 2 T. warm water
2 tsp.	finely grated orange zest (opt.)
¼ c.	orange juice concentrate

Preheat oven to 350 degrees. In a bowl or food processor, whisk together the flour, 3 packets Truvia, baking powder, soda and salt. Cut in the margarine until mixture forms soft crumbs. Transfer to a large mixing bowl. In a small bowl, combine the yogurt, egg replacer, zest and juice concentrate. Add to the dry mix and stir with a spoon until evenly moistened. Mound dough on a non-stick baking sheet (or line a standard baking sheet with parchment paper or a silicone mat). With well-floured hands, pat dough into an even 9-inch round. With a floured knife, cut through dough to make 8 wedges; leave in place on pan. Top with last packet of Truvia. Bake until golden brown, about 25 minutes. Serve hot, or slide onto a cooling rack. Cut into wedges before serving.

Variation:
Use lemon yogurt and lemon zest.

Nutrition Facts

Serving Size (73g)
Servings Per Container

Amount Per Serving

Calories 190   Calories from Fat 45

	% Daily Value*
Total Fat 5g	8%
Saturated Fat 1.5g	8%
Trans Fat 0g	
Cholesterol 0mg	0%
Sodium 250mg	10%
Total Carbohydrate 33g	11%
Dietary Fiber 4g	16%
Sugars 7g	
Protein 4g	

CHAPTER SEVEN

Gluten Gone: Wheat-Free Options

Increasing numbers of people are realizing they have celiac disease or are gluten intolerant, and increasing numbers of gluten-free products are appearing in stores and on restaurant menus. Here, learn how to make flour mixtures that avoid wheat, barley, rye and oats.

Alternate Flours for Gluten-Free Preparations

There are 4 categories of alternate flours:
- Grain flours, including teff, quinoa, sorghum and amaranth.
- Protein flours, including both nut meals (almond, coconut, hazelnut, pecan, etc.) and bean flours, including soy, garfava, garbanzo and other bean flours.
- Starch flours, including rice, tapioca, arrowroot, corn, potato and kudzu.
- Enhancer flours. including vegetable flours, montina, mesquite and buckwheat.

These four types of flour are generally used in combination along with binders which replace the proteins in gluten. Binders include xanthan gum and guar gum.

Purchasing alternate flours is easy. You can find most of them at your local health food store or at Whole Foods Market. Ask your store manager to order them. Or shop online. Store these flours in a dry, dark space or your refrigerator. Their oils make them more perishable and likely to become rancid. Buy in small quantities when possible.

- My favorite flour mixes include a Brown Rice Flour Mix: 2 c. brown rice flour, $\frac{2}{3}$ c. potato starch (NOT potato flour) and $\frac{1}{3}$ c. tapioca starch (or tapioca flour; they are interchangeable, unlike potato starch and potato flour). Brown rice flour imparts a nutty taste and is both heavier and healthier than white rice flours. This mix is great for baking and is most similar to whole wheat flour.
- Almond Flour Mix: 6 c. brown rice flour, 2 c. potato starch (NOT flour),1 c. sweet rice flour, 1 c. tapioca flour/starch, 2 c. whole almonds. Mix well in processor. Delicious and nutritious! Beware of guests' nut allergies.
- Sorghum Flour Mix: 1½ c. sorghum flour, 1½ c. potato starch OR cornstarch, 1 c. tapioca flour/starch. Has a slight molasses-like flavor perfect for baking.
- Corn Flour Mix: 1 c. masa, 1 c. brown rice flour, 1 c. millet OR sorghum, 1 c. cornstarch. Substitute mix for wheat flour and add 1 tsp. xanthan gum per cup of mix. Add an additional egg to recipes for a chewy texture. This has a lovely taste and aroma and wonderful texture when you add the additional egg.

Whether you substitute a flour mix for all-purpose flour or follow a recipe exactly, your gluten-free guests will be very appreciative of your baking efforts. Often no one but you will know it is gluten-free. These recipes can taste that good!

— Carol Nardello

Gluten-Free Anadama Bread

Makes 8-10 slices   *Carol Nardello*

This is a rendition of a New England classic bread which creates a "wheat-y" taste using teff flour with cornmeal and molasses. Delicious for sandwiches, but amazing for toast with apple butter!

⅓ c.	cornmeal
1 c.	boiling water
3 T.	Smart Balance margarine
¼ c.	molasses
2	eggs
2 (¼-oz.)	pckg. quick rise yeast
¾ c.	warm water, divided
2½ c.	Brown Rice Flour Mix (recipe follows)
⅓ c.	teff flour
⅓ c.	cornstarch
⅔ c.	dry milk powder
1 T.	xanthan gum
1 tsp.	salt

In a medium bowl, combine cornmeal and boiling water. Stir in margarine and molasses. Cool. Stir in eggs. Set aside. In a small bowl, dissolve yeast in ¼ c. warm water. Lightly grease a 9-by-5-inch loaf pan. Combine all the dry ingredients in the bowl of a stand mixer. Stir the dissolved yeast into the cornmeal mixture with the remaining ½ c. warm water. Mix until smooth. Pour over dry ingredients and blend to mix for 1 minute. Scrape down the sides of the bowl and mix on high for 5 minutes. Spread batter in prepared pan, and cover with plastic wrap which has been lightly sprayed with cooking spray. Let rise 45-60 minutes or until batter reaches the top of the pan. While bread is rising, preheat oven to 350 degrees. Bake for 55-60 minutes.

Brown Rice Flour Mix: 2 c. brown rice flour, ⅓ c. tapioca starch, ⅔ c. potato starch.

Nutrition Facts

Serving Size (149g)
Servings Per Container

Amount Per Serving

Calories 360   Calories from Fat 80

	% Daily Value*
Total Fat 9g	14%
Saturated Fat 3g	15%
Trans Fat 0.5g	
Cholesterol 55mg	18%
Sodium 420mg	18%
Total Carbohydrate 64g	21%
Dietary Fiber 4g	16%
Sugars 9g	
Protein 8g	

Magical Bread

Serves 8 *Carol Nardello*

This bread more closely resembles wheat-based breads than the vast majority of gluten-free loaves, rising impressively with light, tender and moist texture. The flavor closely resembles wheat bread, too. Like many gluten-free breads, this loaf slices best when cool. Try to wait if you can.

2½ c.	Brown Rice Flour Mix (recipe follows)
⅓ c.	teff flour
⅓ c.	cornstarch
⅔ c.	dry milk powder
1 T.	xanthan gum
1 tsp.	salt
1 (7g)	pckg. active dry yeast
1¾ c.	warm water (110 degrees)
2 T.	molasses or Splenda Brown Sugar
2 T.	vegetable oil
2	eggs

Grease a 9-by-5-inch loaf pan and line with parchment paper. In the bowl of a stand mixer, combine all of the dry ingredients, including the yeast. Add all the wet ingredients and mix for one minute. Scrape down the sides of the bowl and mix on high for 5 minutes. Pour batter into prepared pan and cover loosely with oiled plastic wrap. Allow to rise one hour or until dough reaches the top of the pan. Preheat oven to 350 degrees. Bake for 55-60 minutes. Cool in pan for 10 minutes and remove to wire rack to complete cooling.

Brown Rice Flour mix: 2 c. brown rice flour, ⅔ c. potato starch, ⅓ c. tapioca starch.

Variation:
To make gluten-free "Wannabe Rye Bread," add 3 T. caraway seeds; omit molasses or Splenda Brown Sugar and use instead ½ T. regular Splenda and add ½ tsp. salt.

Nutrition Facts

Serving Size (144g)
Servings Per Container

Amount Per Serving

Calories 320	Calories from Fat 80

	% Daily Value*
Total Fat 9g	14%
Saturated Fat 3g	15%
Trans Fat 0g	
Cholesterol 65mg	22%
Sodium 360mg	15%
Total Carbohydrate 55g	18%
Dietary Fiber 3g	12%
Sugars 7g	
Protein 8g	

Gluten-Free Cornbread

Makes 6 servings *Carol Nardello*

This quickly became a favorite because no one knows it's gluten-free and it's great hot with butter!

½ c.	rice flour
¼ c.	tapioca flour
¼ c.	sorghum flour
¾ c.	cornmeal
2 tsp.	baking powder
1 tsp.	baking soda
½ tsp.	salt
3 T.	Splenda
2	eggs
1 c.	plain yogurt
2 T.	Smart Balance margarine

Preheat oven to 400 degrees. Grease a 9-inch round cake pan. In a large bowl, combine rice flour, tapioca flour, sorghum flour, cornmeal, baking powder, baking soda, Splenda and salt. In a medium bowl, combine eggs, yogurt and margarine (melted). Mix well. Pour combined liquids over dry ingredients. Mix together just until moistened. Pour into prepared pan and bake in hot oven for 20-25 minutes.

Nutrition Facts
Serving Size (94g)
Servings Per Container

Amount Per Serving

Calories 220   Calories from Fat 50

% Daily Value*

Total Fat 6g	9%
Saturated Fat 1.5g	8%
Trans Fat 0.5g	
Cholesterol 75mg	25%
Sodium 880mg	37%
Total Carbohydrate 36g	12%
Dietary Fiber 2g	8%
Sugars 3g	
Protein 7g	

Gluten-Free Graham Crackers

Makes 8-10 slices *Carol Nardello*

These are fabulous for S'Mores or graham cracker crumb crusts.

2 c.	Gluten-Free Flour Mix (recipe follows)
¼ c.	brown rice flour
¼ c.	Splenda Brown Sugar
2 tsp.	cinnamon
1 tsp.	ground ginger
1 tsp.	baking powder
½ tsp.	baking soda
½ tsp.	xanthan gum
½ c.	cold Smart Balance
3 T.	water
3 T.	honey
1 T.	vanilla

Line two sheet trays with parchment paper. Spray paper lightly with vegetable oil cooking spray. Combine flours, Splenda Brown Sugar, spices, baking powder and soda, salt and xanthan gum. Cut in Smart Balance with a pastry blender until mixture is coarse and crumbly. In a small bowl, combine water, honey and vanilla. Pour over crumb mixture and blend until it holds its shape. Adjust with a tiny bit more water or flour as needed. Divide dough in half, wrap tightly and chill 1 hour. Roll chilled dough directly onto lined sheet trays by placing a second sheet of parchment on top. Carefully peel off parchment and score dough with a knife into squares. Remove rough edges of dough. Prick holes all over crackers with a fork. Preheat oven to 325 degrees. Roll scraps of dough into 1-inch balls and flatten onto prepared sheet trays for graham cookies. Prick with fork. Bake crackers and cookies in hot oven for 15-20 minutes or until golden. Remove from oven and re-score cut lines with a knife while still warm. Remove to wire rack to cool.

Gluten-Free Flour Mix:
Combine ⅔ c. garbanzo flour, ⅔ c. tapioca starch, ⅔ c. cornstarch.

Nutrition Facts
Serving Size (73g)
Servings Per Container

Amount Per Serving	
Calories 280	Calories from Fat 90

	% Daily Value*
Total Fat 10g	15%
Saturated Fat 3g	15%
Trans Fat 0g	
Cholesterol 0mg	0%
Sodium 240mg	10%
Total Carbohydrate 42g	14%
Dietary Fiber 3g	12%
Sugars 7g	
Protein 2g	

Gluten-Free Pumpkin Spice Cupcakes with Cream Cheese–Maple Icing

Makes 12 cupcakes *Carol Nardello*

Desserts, soup, breads, even coffee all taste better with pumpkin and spices! This cupcake recipe marries those wonderful pumpkin spice flavors with an amazing maple-flavored cream cheese icing that you must try. Unable to find maple flavoring? Decrease confectioner's sugar to 1 cup and add ¼ cup maple syrup.

½ c.	milk		1 tsp.	vanilla
½ T.	vinegar		2 c.	almond flour mix*
½ c.	Smart Balance margarine		½ tsp.	baking powder
½ c.	Splenda Brown Sugar		1 tsp.	baking soda
1 T.	molasses		½ tsp.	salt
1 T.	honey		1 tsp.	cinnamon
2	eggs		1 tsp.	finely grated fresh ginger
1 c.	canned pumpkin		¼ tsp.	EACH nutmeg and ground cloves

Preheat oven to 350 degrees. Line a 12-cup muffin tin with paper liners. Combine milk and vinegar and let rest 5-10 minutes. With an electric mixer and in a large bowl, cream the margarine, Splenda Brown Sugar, molasses and honey until smooth. Add the eggs and continue beating until light and fluffy. Stir in the pumpkin and vanilla. In a medium bowl, combine the almond flour mix, baking powder, soda, salt, cinnamon, ginger, nutmeg and cloves. Combine the wet and dry ingredients alternately with the milk. Stir until smooth. Avoid overmixing. Spoon batter into prepared pan and bake in hot oven for 25 minutes. Cool well on a wire rack before icing.

*To make almond flour:
Combine 2 c. brown rice flour, ⅓ c. tapioca flour, ½ c. potato starch (not potato flour) and ½ cup finely ground almonds.

Cream Cheese–Maple Icing:
Combine 8 oz. softened cream cheese; 1 tsp. maple flavoring, ¼ c. Smart Balance margarine, 1¼ c. confectioner's sugar in medium bowl and beat until smooth.

Nutrition Facts

Serving Size (108g)
Servings Per Container

Amount Per Serving

Calories 280   Calories from Fat 100

	% Daily Value*
Total Fat 11g	17%
Saturated Fat 2g	10%
Trans Fat 1.5g	
Cholesterol 35mg	12%
Sodium 390mg	16%
Total Carbohydrate 41g	14%
Dietary Fiber 5g	20%
Sugars 3g	
Protein 4g	

Gluten-Free Mango Bread

Makes 8-10 slices *Carol Nardello*

This recipe was devised for a mango festival cooking competition where it was the only gluten-free offering.

1 c.	soy flour		⅓ c.	Smart Balance margarine
½ c.	potato flour		⅓ c.	Splenda Brown Sugar
¼ c.	rice flour		2	eggs
½ tsp.	xanthan gum		½ tsp.	almond extract
1 tsp.	baking soda		1 c.	mangos, diced
1¼ tsp.	cream of tartar		½ c.	chopped walnuts
1½ tsp.	cinnamon		½ c.	flaked coconut
½ tsp.	salt			

Preheat oven to 350 degrees. Grease an 8-by-4-inch loaf pan. In a medium bowl, whisk together the flours, xanthan gum, baking soda, cream of tartar, cinnamon and salt. Set aside. With an electric mixer and in a large mixing bowl, cream margarine and Splenda until light and fluffy. Add the eggs and almond extract. Beat well. Add the combined dry ingredients alternately with the diced mangos. Mix until smooth. Stir in the nuts and coconut and pour into prepared pan. Bake in hot oven for 65 minutes or until a toothpick inserted in the center comes out clean. Cool in pan 15 minutes and invert onto cooling rack. Slices best when completely chilled.

Nutrition Facts

Serving Size (112g)
Servings Per Container

Amount Per Serving

Calories 340   Calories from Fat 120

	% Daily Value*
Total Fat 13g	20%
Saturated Fat 3.5g	18%
Trans Fat 0g	
Cholesterol 70mg	23%
Sodium 450mg	19%
Total Carbohydrate 46g	15%
Dietary Fiber 6g	24%
Sugars 7g	
Protein 10g	

Gluten-Free Banana Bread

Makes 8-10 slices *Carol Nardello*

This was the first recipe I developed after being diagnosed with Celiac. Once it was perfected, I realized that living a gluten-free lifestyle wouldn't be so bad after all. I try to always bake two of these: one for today and one for the freezer (it freezes beautifully).

1 c.	soy flour		⅓ c.	Smart Balance margarine
½ c.	potato flour		½ c.	Splenda
¼ c.	rice flour		2	eggs
½ tsp.	xanthan gum		1 c.	bananas, mashed
1 tsp.	baking soda		1 tsp.	almond extract
1¼ tsp.	cream of tartar		1 tsp.	banana extract
1 tsp.	cinnamon		¼ c.	mini chocolate chips (opt.)
½ tsp.	salt			

Preheat oven to 350 degrees. Grease an 8-by-4-inch loaf pan. In a medium bowl, whisk together flours, xanthan gum, baking soda, cream of tartar, cinnamon and salt. Set aside. Using an electric mixer, beat margarine and Splenda until light and fluffy. Add eggs. Beat well. Add the combined dry ingredients alternately with the banana. Stir in extracts and chocolate chips. Pour into prepared pan. Bake in hot oven for 1 hour or until a toothpick inserted into the center comes out clean. Cool in pan 15 minutes and invert onto a cooling rack. Slices best when completely chilled.

Nutrition Facts

Serving Size (72g)
Servings Per Container

Amount Per Serving

Calories 220   Calories from Fat 100

% Daily Value*

Total Fat 11g	**17%**
Saturated Fat 2.5g	**13%**
Trans Fat 1.5g	
Cholesterol 55mg	**18%**
Sodium 400mg	**17%**
Total Carbohydrate 23g	**8%**
Dietary Fiber 4g	**16%**
Sugars 3g	
Protein 6g	

Gluten-Free Chocolate Spice Cake

Makes 8-10 servings *Carol Nardello*

Chocolate and spice is a natural marriage in this moist, flourless chocolate torte.

15 oz.	garbanzo beans
12 oz.	gluten-free semi-sweet chocolate chips
4	eggs
¾ c.	Splenda
½ tsp.	baking powder
1 tsp.	cinnamon
¼ tsp.	cayenne pepper

Preheat oven to 350 degrees. Grease a 9-inch round cake pan.
For a silky smooth-textured cake, squeeze beans between fingers to release skins and discard skins before rinsing and draining. Place chocolate in small saucepan and melt on low heat, stirring until smooth. Remove from heat and cool. In the bowl of a food processor, combine beans and eggs and process until smooth. In a small bowl, combine Splenda, baking powder, cinnamon and cayenne. Add mixed spices to bean mixture along with cooled, melted chocolate. Blend until smooth. Scrape down sides of food processor bowl to incorporate all of the chocolate, mixing well. Pour into prepared pan and bake for 40 minutes or until knife inserted in the center comes out clean. Cool in pan for 15 minutes or more before inverting onto a serving platter. See if your guests can identify the hidden ingredient.

Nutrition Facts

Serving Size (124g)
Servings Per Container

Amount Per Serving

Calories 290	Calories from Fat 80

	% Daily Value*
Total Fat 9g	**14%**
Saturated Fat 3g	**15%**
Trans Fat 0g	
Cholesterol 110mg	**37%**
Sodium 220mg	**9%**
Total Carbohydrate 44g	**15%**
Dietary Fiber 4g	**16%**
Sugars 17g	
Protein 7g	

Gluten-Free Carrot Cake

Makes 8 slices *Carol Nardello*

Carrot cake, a longtime favorite, is readily made gluten-free and lower fat.

1⅓ c.	brown rice flour
¼ c.	Splenda
½ c.	Splenda Brown Sugar
2 tsp.	baking powder
1 tsp.	xanthan gum
2 tsp.	cinnamon
⅔ c.	unsweetened applesauce
2	eggs
1 tsp.	vanilla
4 med.	carrots, peeled and grated
½ c.	shredded coconut
⅓ c.	crushed pineapple, well drained
¼ c.	raisins

Preheat oven to 350 degrees. Grease and brown-rice-flour 2 mini loaf pans OR 1 (5-by-9-inch) loaf pan. In a large mixing bowl, combine flour, Splendas, baking powder, xanthan gum and cinnamon. In a medium bowl, combine applesauce, eggs and vanilla. Pour liquids over dry ingredients and mix well. Stir in carrots, pineapple and raisins until smooth. Spoon batter into prepared pan(s). Bake for 65 minutes (for large loaf) or until skewer inserted in center comes out clean. Cool completely in pan. Remove from pan, chill, and ice top with cream cheese icing, if desired.

Cream Cheese Icing

4 oz.	fat-free cream cheese
1 T.	Smart Balance margarine
2-3 tsp.	frozen fruit juice concentrate

Whip cream cheese and margarine together until smooth. Add enough fruit juice concentrate (thawed) to create a spreadable consistency. Spread onto chilled loaf cake.

Nutrition Facts

Serving Size (147g)
Servings Per Container

Amount Per Serving

Calories 250   Calories from Fat 50

	% Daily Value*
Total Fat 5g	8%
Saturated Fat 3g	15%
Trans Fat 0g	
Cholesterol 55mg	18%
Sodium 280mg	12%
Total Carbohydrate 44g	15%
Dietary Fiber 4g	16%
Sugars 13g	
Protein 6g	

Gluten-Free Chocolate Pudding Cake

Makes 9 servings *Carol Nardello*

Pudding cake (aka cake-top pudding) is an old-fashioned recipe in which the ingredients mysteriously form a moist cake on top and a pudding on the bottom. Spoon it up like pudding. This could also be baked in individual ramekins.

1 c.	Gluten-Free Flour Mix (recipe follows)
2 T.	cocoa
3 tsp.	baking powder
¼ tsp.	salt
½ c.	brown sugar
½ c.	milk
1½ T.	vegetable oil
2 tsp.	vanilla

For the topping:

½ c.	brown sugar
3 T.	cocoa
1¾ c.	boiling water

Preheat oven to 350 degrees. Lightly grease a 9-inch-square pan. In a large bowl, combine the flour, cocoa, baking powder, salt and brown sugar. Stir in the milk, oil and vanilla until smooth and creamy. Spread evenly into prepared pan. In a small bowl, stir together the brown sugar and cocoa. Sprinkle evenly on top of cake and carefully pour boiling water evenly over the topping. Bake in hot oven for 35 minutes. Cake should invert itself while cooking. Cake layer should spring back when lightly touched in center when done. Remove from oven and cool slightly to serve.

Gluten-Free Flour Mix: Stir together 2½ c. rice flour, 1 c. potato starch flour, 1 c. tapioca flour, ¼ c. cornstarch, ¼ c. garbanzo, cannellini or other bean flour, 2 T. xanthan gum. Place in airtight container and store in freezer. Yields 5 cups.

Nutrition Facts

Serving Size (94g)
Servings Per Container

Amount Per Serving

Calories 220   Calories from Fat 50

	% Daily Value*
Total Fat 6g	9%
Saturated Fat 1.5g	8%
Trans Fat 0.5g	
Cholesterol 75mg	25%
Sodium 880mg	37%
Total Carbohydrate 36g	12%
Dietary Fiber 2g	8%
Sugars 3g	
Protein 7g	

Gluten-Free Peanut Butter Cookies with Guava Jelly

Makes about 24 cookies *Alyssa Moreau*

There is something that brings out the kid in all of us with peanut butter cookies. In this peanut butter and jelly cookie, you can play with the flavors by alternating jams in the filling. Other ideas: crystalized ginger in the batter; making a peanut butter "sandwich" by rolling out the dough between two sheets of parchment then spreading jam on half of the dough, folding over and baking and cutting into bars. (Baking time is a bit longer due to the increased thickness; add about 3-5 minutes)

½ c.	sorghum flour	4 pckts.	Truvia sweetener
½ c.	brown rice flour	2 c.	peanut butter
½ c.	millet flour	½ c.	agave or honey
1 tsp.	baking powder	½ c.	almond milk (or any type of milk)
½ tsp.	baking soda	1 T.	vanilla
½ tsp.	salt	½ c.	guava jelly
½ tsp.	guar gum (or xanthan)		

Preheat oven to 350 degrees. Line a baking sheet with parchment paper. In a medium mixing bowl, combine dry ingredients. In a separate bowl, combine the peanut butter, agave, almond milk and vanilla. You may need to whisk or pulse-blend with a stick blender to incorporate all the ingredients. Add the liquid mixture to the dry and stir until it looks like a thick cookie batter.

Form into balls (about the size of a quarter) and press in the middle with your thumb or small spoon to form an indent. Place on cookie sheet and bake for 10-12 minutes; cookies should be slightly browned around the edges. Cool 5 minutes on rack, then fill cookies with a small spoonful of jelly and transfer to cooling rack.

Variation:

- Omit the jelly and roll the balls in cane sugar, then flatten (criss-cross style) with a fork ; baking time will be a bit shorter, so check at 8-10 minutes.

Nutrition Facts

Serving Size (64g)
Servings Per Container

Amount Per Serving

Calories 200   Calories from Fat 100

	% Daily Value*
Total Fat 11g	17%
Saturated Fat 2g	10%
Trans Fat 0g	
Cholesterol 0mg	0%
Sodium 200mg	8%
Total Carbohydrate 33g	11%
Dietary Fiber 2g	8%
Sugars 12g	
Protein 6g	

Gluten-Free Lilikoi Bars

Makes 12 cookies *Carol Nardello*

A cousin to the old familiar lemon bar, this sweet-tart cookie is an eye-opener. Make lilikoi purée from fresh passionfruit in season, or you can sometimes find it at kitchen supply shops.

For the crust:
- ¼ c. rice flour
- ½ c. brown rice flour
- ¼ c. cornstarch
- ½ tsp. xanthan gum
- ¼ c. powdered sugar
- ½ c. Smart Balance margarine, chilled and cubed
- 2 T. water

For the filling:
- ¾ c. Splenda
- 2 T. brown rice flour
- 2 eggs
- ⅓ c. lilikoi purée*

Make the crust: Preheat oven to 350 degrees. Grease and dust a 8-inch-square pan with rice flour. In the bowl of an electric mixer, combine flours, cornstarch, xanthan gum and powdered sugar. Pulse to blend. Add margarine cubes and water and continue pulsing until dough adheres. Press evenly into prepared pan and bake in hot oven for 35-40 minutes or until golden brown.

Make the filling: In a small bowl, combine Splenda and brown rice flour. Stir in eggs and purée. Mix until smooth and pour over hot crust. Return pan to oven and bake for 15 more minutes or until filling has set. Cool completely before cutting.

* To make lilikoi purée: Halve 24 lilikoi (about 2 pounds) and scoop out the pulp and seeds into a sieve over a large bowl. Rub the pulp through the sieve. Discard the seeds. Sweeten to taste with sugar or artificial sweetener and whisk in a little cornstarch or arrowroot. Over medium-high heat, boil purée, being sure not to burn it. Boil 4-5 minutes, then remove from heat.

Nutrition Facts

Serving Size (12g)
Servings Per Container

Amount Per Serving	
Calories 60	Calories from Fat 35
	% Daily Value*
Total Fat 4g	6%
Saturated Fat 0.5g	3%
Trans Fat 0.5g	
Cholesterol 0mg	0%
Sodium 35mg	1%
Total Carbohydrate 5g	2%
Dietary Fiber 0g	0%
Sugars 1g	
Protein 0g	

Meyer Lemon Cheesecake Squares

Makes 24 servings *Carol Nardello*

Many Islanders have Meyer lemon trees in their yards, or the newer bush-size dwarf varieties. And the fruit are becoming more widely available by means of farmers' markets. Sweeter then conventional lemons, they may fool you at first because before they're fully ripe, they look like large, local limes. They can be used anytime between their tarter celadon phase and the fully ripe yellow-orange color. Here, their acid offsets the richness of cream cheese.

For the crust:
- 3 c. graham cracker crumbs
- 2 tsp. Splenda Brown Sugar
- 4 T. Smart Balance, room temp.
- 2 tsp. vanilla

For the cheesecake:
- ¾ c. all-fruit raspberry preserves
- 3 (8-oz.) blocks cream cheese (less-fat)
- 1½ c. Splenda
- ¼ c. Gluten-Free Flour Mix*
- 4 eggs
- Juice and zest of 3 Meyer lemons

For the garnish:
- ½ pint fresh raspberries
- ½ bunch fresh mint

Preheat oven to 350 degrees. In a food processor, combine graham crumbs and Splenda Brown Sugar. Add the Smart Balance and vanilla and process until crumbs are thoroughly mixed. Press into a 9-by-13-inch pan, using a measuring cup to flatten the crumbs and coat the sides of the pan. Bake 20 minutes or until golden brown. Cool. Spread raspberry preserves evenly on cooled crust.

In a large bowl with an electric mixer, combine cream cheese, Splenda and flour, beating until fluffy. Add eggs, lemon zest and juice just until blended (avoid overmixing). Carefully spread over raspberry preserves and bake for 40-45 minutes or until center is almost set. Cool on wire rack. Cover and refrigerate. Cut into 24 squares. Garnish each square with a raspberry and mint leaf.

*Gluten-Free Flour Mix: ⅔ cup EACH garbanzo flour, tapioca starch and cornstarch.

Nutrition Facts

Serving Size (76g)
Servings Per Container

Amount Per Serving

Calories 180	Calories from Fat 80
	% Daily Value*
Total Fat 8g	12%
Saturated Fat 4g	20%
Trans Fat 0g	
Cholesterol 50mg	17%
Sodium 170mg	7%
Total Carbohydrate 21g	7%
Dietary Fiber 0g	0%
Sugars 10g	
Protein 5g	

Ultimate Chocolate Supreme Cookies

Makes 24 cookies *Carol Nardello*

This recipe might end up being the most delicious gluten-free cookie you'll ever eat. It combines two favorite flavors: chocolate and salt.

¾ c.	brown rice flour
½ c.	sorghum flour
½ c.	tapioca starch
⅓ c.	cocoa powder
½ tsp.	baking soda
¾ tsp.	coarse salt, divided
½ tsp.	xanthan gum
½ c.	Smart Balance margarine, softened
⅔ c.	Splenda Brown Sugar
¼ c.	sugar
2	eggs
1½ tsp.	vanilla
¾ c.	mini chocolate chips

In a medium bowl, combine flours, cocoa powder, baking soda, ½ tsp. salt and xanthan gum. In a large mixing bowl, cream margarine with sugars. Add eggs and vanilla and continue beating until light and fluffy. Add combined dry ingredients and mix until incorporated. Stir in chips. Cover and chill dough.

Preheat oven to 350 degrees. Line sheet trays with parchment paper and use a mini ice cream scoop or teaspoon to form cookies from chilled dough, leaving space between for spreading. Press to flatten. Garnish cookies with a sprinkle of the remaining coarse salt. Bake in hot oven for 10-12 minutes. Cool in the pan.

Nutrition Facts

Serving Size (31g)
Servings Per Container

Amount Per Serving

Calories 130   Calories from Fat 60

% Daily Value*

Total Fat 6g	9%
Saturated Fat 2g	10%
Trans Fat 0.5g	
Cholesterol 20mg	7%
Sodium 140mg	6%
Total Carbohydrate 17g	6%
Dietary Fiber 1g	4%
Sugars 2g	
Protein 2g	

Gluten-Free Raspberry–Coconut Bars

Makes 16 servings *Carol Nardello*

Who says cookies are a closed book when you can't have wheat? Here's a luxurious bar cookie that won't leave anyone feeling deprived.

For the crust:
1 c.	Gluten-Free Flour Mix (recipe follows)
2 tsp.	baking powder
1 T.	sugar
½ c.	butter, softened
2	eggs, beaten
1 T.	milk

For the filling:
½ c.	raspberry jam (sugar-free or fruit-only, if desired)
1 tsp.	almond extract

For the topping:
1	egg
4 T.	butter, melted
1 tsp.	vanilla
1 c.	sugar
2 c.	shredded coconut

Preheat oven to 350 degrees. Lightly grease or oil-spray a 9-inch-square pan. In a medium bowl, combine flour, baking powder and sugar. Cut in butter until crumbly throughout. Stir in eggs and milk until smooth. With floured hands, pat dough evenly into the bottom of the prepared pan. In a small bowl, combine jam and extract and spread over crust. In a medium bowl, combine the egg, butter and vanilla. Stir in the sugar and coconut until well mixed. Spread carefully over jam layer. Bake in hot oven for 30 minutes or until topping is golden brown. Cool in pan and cut into 16 pieces.

Gluten-Free Flour Mix:

Combine 2½ c. rice flour, 1 c. potato starch flour, 1 c. tapioca flour, ¼ c. cornstarch, ¼ c. bean flour, 2 T. xanthan gum and store in air-tight container. Store in freezer. Yields 5 cups.

Nutrition Facts

Serving Size (59g)
Servings Per Container

Amount Per Serving	
Calories 210	Calories from Fat 120
	% Daily Value*
Total Fat 14g	22%
Saturated Fat 9g	45%
Trans Fat 0g	
Cholesterol 65mg	22%
Sodium 115mg	5%
Total Carbohydrate 24g	8%
Dietary Fiber 1g	4%
Sugars 15g	
Protein 2g	

Gluten-Free Pancakes with Blueberry Sauce

Makes 6-8 servings — *Carol Nardello*

Pancakes and blueberries—a natural pairing. And blueberries are rich in cancer-fighting antioxidants.

For the pancakes:

1 c.	milk
1 T.	vinegar
1 c.	brown rice flour
½ c.	cornstarch
½ c.	rice flour
¼ c.	Splenda
1 T.	baking powder
½ tsp.	salt
¼ tsp.	xanthan gum
2	eggs, beaten
¼ c.	vegetable oil
1 tsp.	vanilla
⅓ c.	water, as needed

For the blueberry sauce:

2 c.	blueberries, fresh or frozen
½	lemon, zested and juiced
2 T.	cornstarch
½ c.	cold water
⅓ c.	Splenda
½ tsp.	vanilla
⅛ tsp.	cinnamon

Make the sauce: In a saucepan over medium heat, combine berries, zest, juice and Splenda. Bring to a boil. In a small bowl, mix cornstarch, cinnamon and water together until smooth. Add to boiling berries and stir until smooth and slightly thickened. Remove from heat and stir in vanilla. Keep warm.

Make the pancakes: In a small bowl, combine milk and vinegar. Set aside 5 minutes. Combine dry ingredients in a large bowl. Combine milk mixture with eggs, oil and vanilla. Pour egg mixture over dry ingredients and stir to blend well. Stir in water to thin. Preheat griddle over medium heat. Pour batter into oiled pan. Cook approximately 3 minutes per side or until bubbles appear all over. Flip over and cook 2-3 minutes more. Serve with Blueberry Sauce.

Nutrition Facts

Serving Size (154g)
Servings Per Container

Amount Per Serving

Calories 280   Calories from Fat 90

	% Daily Value*
Total Fat 10g	15%
Saturated Fat 2g	10%
Trans Fat 0g	
Cholesterol 55mg	18%
Sodium 380mg	16%
Total Carbohydrate 42g	14%
Dietary Fiber 2g	8%
Sugars 5g	
Protein 5g	

CHAPTER EIGHT

Have Your Cake and Eat It Too!

Cakes are definitely treat-only, eat-occasionally food.
But they can be made healthier and even more interesting
through the use of fresh and dried fruit and nuts, alternative flours
and sweeteners, and lowfat dairy ingredients.

Easy Lemon Tiramisu

Makes 8 servings *Sharon Kobayashi*

This is an easy, refreshing way to impress guests. Italian ladyfingers and Limoncello, a lemon liqueur, can be found at gourmet food stores such as R. Field and in some supermarkets. Stored in a zippered plastic bag, ladyfingers will keep for a long time. Local thin-skinned lemons are sweeter than their mainland relatives, so less sugar and fat are necessary to balance this tangy citrus fruit. Pasteurized powdered egg whites (available at kitchen stores and in the baking aisle of some supermarkets) work well in this recipe.

2 T.	lemon juice (local thin-skinned lemons, or Meyer lemons)
½ tsp.	lemon zest
3 T.	powdered sugar
1 c.	lowfat ricotta cheese
1 tsp.	unflavored gelatin
2 T.	water
3	egg whites (or pasteurized powdered egg white)
1 c.	light whipped topping
12	ladyfingers, the hard Italian kind
2 T.	Limoncello

In a food processor, combine lemon juice, zest, 2 T. powdered sugar and ricotta. Process till smooth. In a microwavable bowl, sprinkle gelatin over water; let sit 5 minutes. Microwave gelatin 20-30 seconds, or until dissolved. Beat egg whites with 1 T. powdered sugar until soft peaks form. Drizzle in gelatin and mix until incorporated. Mix half the whipped topping with ricotta mixture. Fold in egg whites. In a 1-lb. loaf pan sprayed with cooking spray, spread ⅓ of mixture. Lay half the lady fingers down, breaking off and reserving excess pieces. Sprinkle these with 1 T. Limoncello, then add another ⅓ of mixture. Repeat layers, ending with mixture. Top with remaining whipped topping. Cover with plastic wrap and refrigerate overnight. Crumble remaining ladyfinger pieces over loaf before serving.

Nutrition Facts

Serving Size (128g)
Servings Per Container

Amount Per Serving

Calories 170   Calories from Fat 35

% Daily Value*

Total Fat 4g	6%
Saturated Fat 2.5g	13%
Trans Fat 0g	
Cholesterol 45mg	15%
Sodium 150mg	6%
Total Carbohydrate 19g	6%
Dietary Fiber 0g	0%
Sugars 6g	
Protein 11g	

Carrot and Spice Cupcakes with Pineapple–Cream Cheese Frosting

Makes 12 cupcakes   Sharon Kobayashi

In these cupcakes, the spices, carrots and whole wheat flour lend a slight bitterness. If that bothers you, substitute all-purpose flour. Either way, the carrots and raisins produce a light, moist cupcake. While cooling, the cupcakes will sink a little, which makes a perfect "container" for the frosting.

1½ c.	white whole wheat flour	6 T.	raisins
1½ tsp.	baking powder	1 c.	lowfat buttermilk
¼ c.	light brown sugar	1 T.	lemon juice
2 T.	canola oil	1 c.	grated carrot (packed down)
2	eggs	¾ c.	Pineapple Cream Cheese Frosting
½ c.	egg substitute		(recipe follows)
1 tsp.	pumpkin pie spice	Optional:	1 T. minced candied ginger
½ tsp.	cinnamon		

Preheat oven to 350 degrees. In a medium bowl, whisk together the flours, baking powder and sugar. In another mixing bowl, combine oil, eggs and egg substitute. In a blender, blend the spices, raisins and buttermilk until raisins are broken down (reduced to flecks of black). With an electric mixer, beat egg mixture on high till fluffy and doubled in volume (about 3 minutes). With mixer on low, beat in flour mixture in thirds and buttermilk mixture and lemon juice in halves (begin and end with flour). Fold in carrot and candied ginger, if using. Divide batter evenly among 12 prepared muffin cups. Bake for 35-40 minutes or until a toothpick inserted emerges clean. Cool completely before frosting and store frosted cupcakes in the refrigerator. Decorate with candied ginger, if desired.

Pineapple–Cream Cheese Frosting

¼ c.	fresh minced pineapple
1 T.	water
6 T.	fat-free cream cheese, softened
4 T.	light cream cheese, softened
5 T.	powdered sugar
1 tsp.	vanilla

In a preheated non-stick sauté pan, cook pineapple with 1 T. water. When all liquid evaporates (3-5 minutes), transfer pineapple to a bowl. When pineapple is cool, add remaining ingredients. Whisk together until incorporated. Refrigerate 2-4 hours to set. Makes 12 (1-tablespoon) servings.

Nutrition Facts

Serving Size (83g)
Servings Per Container

Amount Per Serving

Calories 160   Calories from Fat 70

	% Daily Value*
Total Fat 8g	**12%**
Saturated Fat 3.5g	**18%**
Trans Fat 0g	
Cholesterol 50mg	**17%**
Sodium 180mg	**8%**
Total Carbohydrate 17g	**6%**
Dietary Fiber 1g	**4%**
Sugars 11g	
Protein 4g	

Chocolate–Beet Cake with Chocolate Glaze

Makes 9 servings   *Sharon Kobayashi*

Honey, beets and raisins help make this a very moist, rich-tasting cake. Roast fresh, local beets and serve them for dinner one day; use leftovers to make dessert the next. The slight bitterness of whole wheat complements the chocolate well.

1 c.	whole wheat flour	½ c.	egg substitute
½ c.	unsweetened cocoa powder	⅓ c.	red beets, roasted, peeled and grated (about 3 oz.)
½ tsp.	baking soda		
⅛ tsp.	salt	¼ c.	raisins, packed
2 T.	canola oil	1 T.	vanilla extract
3 T.	honey	¾ c.	buttermilk, divided
1 tsp.	molasses	5 oz.	Chocolate Glaze (recipe follows)
1	egg		

Preheat oven to 325. In a medium mixing bowl, whisk together flour, cocoa, baking soda and salt. In a separate large bowl, beat together oil, honey, molasses, eggs and egg substitute till doubled in volume (about 5 minutes). In a blender, combine beets, raisins, vanilla and ½ c. buttermilk; blend until smooth. Remove and set aside. Add last ¼ c. of buttermilk to blender and blend, then add to purée. Add flour mixture in thirds and buttermilk mixture in halves to the egg mixture, starting and ending with flour, mixing until incorporated after each addition. Pour batter into a non-stick 8-by-8-inch baking pan. Bake for 45 minutes or until a toothpick inserted comes out clean, turning pan halfway through baking. Cool completely and serve immediately, or wrap and refrigerate or freeze.

Chocolate Glaze

2 tsp.	unsweetened cocoa powder
¼ c.	lowfat milk
2 oz.	semi-sweet chocolate chips (rounded ⅓ cup)
3 T.	light cream cheese
	Pinch cinnamon
1 tsp.	vanilla extract

Whisk cocoa powder with milk till smooth. Microwave on high until the mixture just starts to boil. Whisk again, add chocolate chips and let sit 2 minutes. Add cream cheese, cinnamon and vanilla. Whisk till smooth; chill. Stir occasionally until thickened. Spread evenly on cake.

Nutrition Facts

Serving Size (128g)
Servings Per Container

Amount Per Serving

Calories 170	Calories from Fat 35

	% Daily Value*
Total Fat 4g	6%
Saturated Fat 2.5g	13%
Trans Fat 0g	
Cholesterol 45mg	15%
Sodium 150mg	6%
Total Carbohydrate 19g	6%
Dietary Fiber 0g	0%
Sugars 6g	
Protein 11g	

Strawberry Gelatin Cake

Makes 9 servings *Sharon Kobayashi*

Homemade strawberry gelatin makes a tasty and lower-sugar topping for this potluck favorite. The gelatin also helps keep the cake moist. If you don't have white whole wheat flour, substitute ⅓ c. whole wheat and ⅔ c. all-purpose flours. Perfect with local strawberries from Kula, Maui, or elsewhere.

1 c.	white whole wheat flour	2	eggs
1 tsp.	baking powder	½ c.	egg substitute
⅛ tsp.	salt	1 tsp.	unflavored gelatin
1 sml.	apple banana, not too ripe, mashed	½ c.	no-added-sugar cranberry juice
½ c.	lowfat buttermilk		(or cranberry–pomegranate)
1 T.	canola oil	1½ c.	quartered Kula strawberries
1 tsp.	vanilla	1½ c.	fat-free whipped topping
3 T.	sugar		

Preheat oven to 350 degrees. In a medium bowl, whisk together flour, baking powder and salt. In another bowl, combine mashed banana, buttermilk, oil and vanilla. Set aside. In a mixing bowl, combine eggs, egg substitute and sugar. Beat on high until pale yellow and tripled in volume (about 5 minutes). Switch mixer to low. Add flour mixture in thirds and buttermilk mixture in halves (start and end with flour). Pour batter into a non-stick 8-inch-by-8-inch pan and bake for 40 minutes or until golden brown. Cool slightly, then poke holes all over the cake with a chopstick (use the fat side).

In a heavy-bottomed saucepan, combine gelatin with cold juice and let sit for 5 minutes. Heat till juice simmers and gelatin dissolves. Add strawberries. Turn off heat, cover pot and let sit 5 minutes or till strawberries are tender. Pour gelatin over cake, distributing strawberries evenly over the top. Refrigerate until chilled, then spread evenly with whipped topping.

Nutrition Facts

Serving Size (120g)
Servings Per Container

Amount Per Serving

Calories 160   Calories from Fat 30

% Daily Value*

Total Fat 3.5g	5%
Saturated Fat 0.5g	3%
Trans Fat 0g	
Cholesterol 50mg	17%
Sodium 160mg	7%
Total Carbohydrate 26g	9%
Dietary Fiber 3g	12%
Sugars 10g	
Protein 6g	

No-Bake Cheesecake

Makes 8-10 servings *Sharon Kobayashi*

Lowfat cottage cheese is the base of this surprisingly rich-tasting cheesecake. Serve with fresh seasonal fruit such as mango, poha or berries.

½ c.	unsalted cracker crumbs
2 T.	unsalted butter
3	pitted medjool dates
¼ tsp.	cinnamon
½ c.	lowfat milk
3 tsp.	unflavored gelatin
2 lb.	lowfat cottage cheese (3½ c.)
¾ c.	sifted powdered sugar
½ tsp.	lemon zest (zest of ½ lemon)
2 tsp.	vanilla extract

In a food processor, combine cracker crumbs, butter, dates and cinnamon. Pulse until combined and mixture sticks together when pressed between your fingers. If mixture does not stick together when pressed, add a few drops of water. Spray a 9-inch round cake pan with cooking spray. Firmly and evenly press crust into bottom of pan. Refrigerate or freeze until firmly set. Combine milk and gelatin and microwave 20-30 seconds or until dissolved. In a food processor, combine cheese, sugar, zest and vanilla, and puree until smooth. With food processor running, drizzle in gelatin mixture. Pour into prepared piecrust and refrigerate overnight.

Nutrition Facts

Serving Size (107g)
Servings Per Container

Amount Per Serving

Calories 130   Calories from Fat 30

	% Daily Value*
Total Fat 3.5g	5%
Saturated Fat 2g	10%
Trans Fat 0g	
Cholesterol 10mg	3%
Sodium 280mg	12%
Total Carbohydrate 19g	6%
Dietary Fiber 1g	4%
Sugars 16g	
Protein 9g	

Healthy Applesauce–Spice Cake

Makes 10 servings   *Carol Nardello*

Picture a cinnamony apple upside-down cake containing no oil, butter or sugar that tastes as good as it looks!

1	apple, peeled, cored and thinly sliced
2½ c.	flour
1 tsp.	baking powder
1 tsp.	baking soda
1 tsp.	cinnamon
1 tsp.	ground ginger
½ tsp.	nutmeg
½ tsp.	salt
2	eggs
1½ c.	unsweetened applesauce
¾ c.	apple juice concentrate
1½ tsp.	vanilla
½ c.	walnuts, chopped

Preheat oven to 350 degrees. Grease an 11-inch tart pan OR a 9-inch springform pan. Line the bottom with parchment paper. Arrange apple slices attractively in a spiral on the pan's bottom. Sift together the flour, baking powder, baking soda, spices and salt. Beat the eggs with the applesauce, apple juice concentrate and vanilla. Add the liquids to the sifted dry ingredients and beat until smooth. Stir in nuts and pour over apples in prepared pan. Bake for 60 minutes or until a toothpick inserted in the center comes out clean.

Nutrition Facts

Serving Size (98g)
Servings Per Container

Amount Per Serving

Calories 180   Calories from Fat 35

% Daily Value*

Total Fat 4g	6%
Saturated Fat 0.5g	3%
Trans Fat 0g	
Cholesterol 35mg	12%
Sodium 260mg	11%
Total Carbohydrate 32g	11%
Dietary Fiber 2g	8%
Sugars 12g	
Protein 4g	

CHAPTER NINE

It's a Jungle Out There: Cooking with Island Fruit

Fresh and dried fruits are natural sweeteners. These recipes make the most of them, especially the tropical fruits of the Islands. Note the many variations and substitutions for these versatile dishes.

Black Fruit Tart

Makes 8 servings *Sharon Kobayashi*

This is a great dessert for late summer or early fall, when grapes and blackberries are in season. Earlier in the summer, try using sweet green or red grapes, raspberries (and raspberry jam) and peaches or red plums or jaboticaba (aka Brazilian grape, found at some farmer's markets and at nurseries, such as Frankie's on O'ahu, that specialize in rare fruits). The oat crust is a building block recipe you can use for other pies or tarts.

10 oz.	Oat Pie Crust (recipe follows)	1 c.	sweet, black, seedless grapes, halved
1 T.	cornstarch	1 c.	fresh or frozen blackberries (substitute frozen pitted dark cherries)
¼ c.	water		
½ tsp.	fresh ginger, grated		
2 T.	blackberry jelly or seedless jam (substitute blueberry jam)	1 c.	black plums, diced (substitute fresh or frozen blueberries)

Preheat oven to 400 degrees. Prepare pie crust as directed. Roll out dough between 2 pieces of plastic wrap to 10 inches in diameter. Use the bottom piece to transfer dough to a 10-inch tart pan sprayed with cooking spray. Center the dough and press into pan, coming up about ⅓ up the sides. Bake for 20 minutes or until golden brown; cool completely.

Mix cornstarch and water; set aside. Place ginger, fruit and jelly in a heavy-bottomed saucepan. Cook over medium-high heat until bubbly. Stir in cornstarch slurry. When juices are thick and clear, remove from heat (approx. 2 minutes). Immediately pour into crust, spreading fruit evenly. Cool completely before serving.

Oat flour makes this crust pleasantly crumbly and crisp. Adding eggs and ricotta cheese gives it moisture and structure. Oat flour can be found at natural food stores, and is also available at some supermarkets in the baking or natural foods aisle. This crust is best for pies and tarts in which the filling and crust are prepared separately (i.e., a gelled or pudding pie).

Nutrition Facts

Serving Size (107g)
Servings Per Container

Amount Per Serving

Calories 180   Calories from Fat 45

% Daily Value*

Total Fat 5g	8%
Saturated Fat 1g	5%
Trans Fat 0g	
Cholesterol 30mg	10%
Sodium 120mg	5%
Total Carbohydrate 27g	9%
Dietary Fiber 3g	12%
Sugars 11g	
Protein 4g	

Oat Pie Crust

¾ c.	oat flour
½ c.	all-purpose flour
¼ tsp.	salt
1 T.	sugar
½ tsp.	baking powder
1 lg.	egg
2 T.	part-skim ricotta cheese
2 T.	vegetable oil

Combine flours, salt, sugar and baking powder in a mixing bowl and whisk to combine. Add egg, cheese and oil; stir. If dough is too dry, sprinkle cautiously with a little water. Dough should be soft but not sticky. Wrap with plastic wrap; set aside for at least 5 minutes before using.

Blueberry and Lemon Cobbler

Makes 4 servings *Sharon Kobayashi*

Cornmeal is a great whole grain to use in desserts. It adds a pleasant nutty flavor without bitterness and great texture, too. Lemon zest brightens the flavor without adding more sugar. This versatile recipe is as easy to do for 8 people as it is for 2, and is a comforting end to a chilly night.

2 c.	blueberries (or mixed berries, plums, peaches, poha, mango—fresh or frozen)
4 tsp.	sugar
¼ c.	cornmeal
2 T.	whole wheat flour
¼ tsp.	baking powder
⅛ tsp.	salt
4 tsp.	butter, unsalted
½ tsp.	finely grated lemon zest
4 tsp.	honey
¼ c.	buttermilk

Preheat oven to 350 degrees. Spray 4 (½-c.) oven-safe ramekins with cooking spray. Place ½ c. berries in each ramekin and sprinkle with 1 tsp. sugar. In a small mixing bowl, combine cornmeal, flour, baking powder and salt. Mix in butter using fingers or cut in with a knife (small lumps are okay). Add lemon zest, honey and buttermilk, stirring to combine. Add an equal amount of topping (about 2 T.) to each ramekin. Bake for 30-40 minutes or until bubbly and golden brown on top. Cool slightly, and serve warm or at room temperature.

Nutrition Facts

Serving Size (118g)
Servings Per Container

Amount Per Serving

Calories 160 Calories from Fat 40

	% Daily Value*
Total Fat 4.5g	7%
Saturated Fat 2.5g	13%
Trans Fat 0g	
Cholesterol 10mg	3%
Sodium 230mg	10%
Total Carbohydrate 31g	10%
Dietary Fiber 3g	12%
Sugars 18g	
Protein 2g	

Date and Macadamia Nut Bars

Makes 12 servings   *Sharon Kobayashi*

Use the oat pie crust to make this updated version of the classic. Medjool dates are sweeter, softer and more flavorful than the more common Deglet Noor dates, so less sugar (and fat) is necessary. Maple syrup adds sweetness and great flavor. Look for medjool dates in natural food stores, and seasonally (fall and winter) at Costco and some grocery stores.

10 oz.	Oat Pie Crust (pg. 111)
14	medjool dates, pitted
⅓ c.	lightly salted macadamia nuts
1	egg
¼ c.	egg substitute
3 T.	real maple syrup
1 T.	vanilla extract
2 T.	all-purpose flour

Preheat oven to 350 degrees. Prepare pie crust as directed. Pat into a non-stick 8-by-8-inch pan, coming up the edges about ½ inch. Use a little of the egg substitute to brush crust, including sides. Make sure to coat the entire crust or the filling will leak down. Bake 30 minutes or until golden brown. Cool.

In a food processor, combine dates, egg, egg substitute, syrup, vanilla and flour. Pulse-chop until dates are broken down, but still have texture. Add nuts and pulse 3-4 more times to chop. Carefully pour onto crust, avoiding overflow on sides. Bake for 30-40 minutes or until golden brown. Cool slightly before cutting. Cool thoroughly before serving.

Nutrition Facts

Serving Size (71g)
Servings Per Container

Amount Per Serving	
Calories 230	Calories from Fat 60

	% Daily Value*
Total Fat 7g	11%
Saturated Fat 1.5g	8%
Trans Fat 0g	
Cholesterol 35mg	12%
Sodium 95mg	4%
Total Carbohydrate 37g	12%
Dietary Fiber 3g	12%
Sugars 23g	
Protein 4g	

Tarte Tatin

Makes 8 servings *Sharon Kobayashi*

Caramelizing the fruit in this upside-down apple tart concentrates the sugars and gives great depth of flavor. Take time to arrange the fruit for a very finished, elegant presentation. Serve it with a dollop of tart plain Greek yogurt, if desired.

6 oz.	Honey Whole Wheat dough (p. 59)
1 T.	butter
2 T.	brown sugar
¼ tsp.	cinnamon
	Pinch allspice
1 c.	starfruit, sliced thin
	(substitute plums or pluots)
1 c.	apples, peeled and sliced thin
	(substitute peaches or nectarines)

Preheat oven to 400 degrees. Prepare dough (as directed in recipe). Spray a 9-inch cake pan with cooking spray. Add butter to pan and place in oven briefly to melt. Swirl pan to coat and sprinkle with sugar, cinnamon and allspice. Arrange fruit in an attractive spiral in pan (remember, the bottom will become the top). Bake for 30 minutes, or until juices start to reduce. Roll dough between 2 pieces of plastic wrap to 9 inches in diameter. Remove pan from oven. Top fruit with crust, using a butter knife to push edges under. Bake for 15-20 minutes or until crust is golden brown. While still warm, flip tart over onto a serving plate.

Nutrition Facts

Serving Size (125g)
Servings Per Container

Amount Per Serving

Calories 140	Calories from Fat 40

	% Daily Value*
Total Fat 4.5g	7%
Saturated Fat 1.5g	8%
Trans Fat 0g	
Cholesterol 5mg	2%
Sodium 100mg	4%
Total Carbohydrate 24g	8%
Dietary Fiber 3g	12%
Sugars 10g	
Protein 3g	

Fruit Summer Rolls with Mint and Lime

Makes 12 servings *Sharon Kobayashi*

This is basically a fruit salad you can eat with your fingers. Vary the fruit according to the season, but be sure to choose ripe but firm fruit, or the rolls become mushy. Also avoid fruit with colors that run, such as dragon fruit. These rolls will hold refrigerated for several hours, making them a convenient party item.

⅓ c.	water
	Juice and zest of 1 lime
3 T.	sugar
½ tsp.	cornstarch mixed with 1 T. water (slurry)
2 T.	unsalted butter
12	rice paper wrappers
6	strawberries, cut in half, sliced thin
1	mango, peeled, cut into ¼-inch-thick sticks
2 lg.	Asian pears, peeled, cored, cut into matchsticks
36	fresh mint leaves

In a saucepan, combine lime zest, 1 T. lime juice (juice of ½ lime) and sugar. (Toss the remaining lime juice with the pear as soon as you cut it to prevent browning.) Bring lime–sugar mixture to a boil. Stir in cornstarch slurry, bring to a second boil and remove from heat. Swirl in butter until melted. Cool mixture completely in refrigerator. To assemble rolls, fill a wide bowl or basin with warm water. Holding a wrapper in both hands, quickly dip it through the water. Lay it on a dry cutting board. On bottom third of wrapper, lay down a line of fruit, working right to left; about ½ cup of fruit total. The pear should predominate. Leave a 2" margin on right, left and side nearest you. Place 3 mint leaves atop the fruit and fold wrapper over fruit on the side closest to you. Fold left and right sides of wrapper over fruit. Finish by rolling up (away from you), keeping the wrap as tight as possible. Rest briefly (without touching) on a silicon sheet or parchment paper (a surface to which the rice paper will not adhere). Cover rolls with damp paper towels and refrigerate if not serving immediately.

Variations: Substitute raspberries or poha for strawberries; persimmon for mango; jicama for Asian pear.

Nutrition Facts

Serving Size (100g)
Servings Per Container

Amount Per Serving

Calories 100	Calories from Fat 20
	% Daily Value*
Total Fat 2.5g	4%
Saturated Fat 1g	5%
Trans Fat 0g	
Cholesterol 5mg	2%
Sodium 10mg	0%
Total Carbohydrate 19g	6%
Dietary Fiber 2g	8%
Sugars 7g	
Protein 1g	

Fruit Parfaits with Yogurt

Makes 12 servings *Sharon Kobayashi*

Anticipate how lovely this dessert can be before you even taste it. The visual appeal of a tasty layered fruit dessert is remarkable. Using honey instead of sugar to sweeten is a healthy choice that children enjoy very much.

3 pints	fresh berries or other cut-up bite-size fruits such as banana, apple, cantaloupe, honeydew, papaya, mango or such tropical fruit as longan, rambutan, dragonfruit, jaboticaba, starfruit or mangosteen
3 c.	plain, fat-free yogurt
½ c.	honey
½ c.	crushed whole grain snack puffs or cereal

Divide fruit equally among 12 clear plastic cups. Top with ¼ cup of yogurt. Drizzle with honey to sweeten. Sprinkle crumbs on top. Eat immediately while topping is still crunchy.

Nutrition Facts
Serving Size (153g)
Servings Per Container

Amount Per Serving	
Calories 140	Calories from Fat 5
	% Daily Value*
Total Fat 0.5g	1%
Saturated Fat 0g	0%
Trans Fat 0g	
Cholesterol 0mg	0%
Sodium 60mg	3%
Total Carbohydrate 30g	10%
Dietary Fiber 1g	4%
Sugars 27g	
Protein 4g	

Tropical Fruit Pie

Makes 6 pieces *Sharon Kobayashi*

This makes a dramatic meal-ender. When they ask what's for dessert, say pizza.

For the crust:

½ c.	almonds
½ c.	shredded fresh or dried or sweetened coconut
1 c.	dates, pitted and chopped
	Dash salt
½ tsp.	vanilla

For the haupia filling:

¾ c.	coconut milk
¾ c.	water
2T.+¾ tsp.	arrowroot
	Sweetener to taste*
⅛ tsp.	salt
¼-in.	piece ginger, peeled, mashed
1 sprig	mint for garnish (optional)
	Fruit for topping

To make the crust: Combine all ingredients in a food processor and blend until a dough-like consistency forms. Pat into an oiled pie plate.

For the haupia: Whisk together all ingredients in a (cool) small cooking pot. Place on stove and bring to a boil, stirring constantly. When thick, remove from heat (remove ginger piece) and pour into prepared crust. Cool at least 2 hours, preferably overnight. Decorate with fruit of choice. Garnish with sprig of mint in center.

Fruit suggestions: pineapple, kiwi, mango, banana, orange, strawberries, blueberries, grapes or any combination.

*4 packets Truvia or ¼ c. agave or honey

Nutrition Facts

Serving Size (82g)
Servings Per Container

Amount Per Serving

Calories 200   Calories from Fat 120

	% Daily Value*
Total Fat 13g	20%
Saturated Fat 8g	40%
Trans Fat 0g	
Cholesterol 0mg	0%
Sodium 80mg	3%
Total Carbohydrate 23g	8%
Dietary Fiber 3g	12%
Sugars 15g	
Protein 3g	

Melon and Mint Sorbet

Makes 8 (½-cup) servings *Sharon Kobayashi*

No ice cream maker necessary for this rich-tasting sorbet. The alcohol and frequent whisking during the freezing process break up the ice crystals and keep the mixture from freezing too hard. Egg whites also aid in a softer texture. Powdered egg whites are pasteurized and work well in this recipe. For best results, let the sorbet stand 3-5 minutes at room temperature after scooping before eating.

½ c.	part-skim ricotta cheese
¼ c.	sugar (sweeten to taste)
3 T.	citrus-flavored vodka (or plain vodka)
8 oz.	honeydew melon, puréed (about 1 c.)
3 oz.	avocado (creamy, string-free variety), about ½ large
3 sprigs	mint, leaves only
3	egg whites
1 T.	sugar
½ tsp.	unflavored gelatin
1 T.	water

In a food processor, process ricotta cheese, vodka and ¼ c. sugar until smooth. Add melon and avocado and process until smooth. Add mint and pulse to chop. Transfer to a mixing bowl (make sure it's one that fits in the freezer). Freeze for 30 minutes, remove and whip for 2-3 minutes. Repeat freezing and whipping process over the next 3 hours (6 times). You can continue for another hour or two if a finer grain is desired. Sprinkle gelatin over water and let sit 5 minutes. Microwave 20-30 seconds, or until gelatin is dissolved. Whip egg whites and 2 T. sugar to soft peaks. Drizzle gelatin mixture into egg whites and mix to incorporate. Beat melon mixture once more, mix in ⅓ of the whites. Gently fold in remaining whites and freeze solid.

Nutrition Facts

Serving Size (82g)
Servings Per Container

Amount Per Serving

Calories 200   Calories from Fat 120

	% Daily Value*
Total Fat 13g	20%
Saturated Fat 8g	40%
Trans Fat 0g	
Cholesterol 0mg	0%
Sodium 80mg	3%
Total Carbohydrate 23g	8%
Dietary Fiber 3g	12%
Sugars 15g	
Protein 3g	

Original Sunrise Smoothie

Makes 2 servings *Sharon Kobayashi*

It is important to use sweet, ripe, fresh papaya for this refreshing smoothie. Use fresh; freezing papaya accentuates the musky character of the fruit, making it disagreeable.

2 T.	quick oats
½ c.	lowfat milk
½	papaya, very ripe
1 lg.	banana, frozen
1 T.	orange juice concentrate
1 tsp.	vanilla extract
4	ice cubes
2 T.	fat-free whipped topping

Soak the oats in the milk for 30 minutes in the refrigerator. Seed and peel papaya.
Combine oats, milk, papaya, orange concentrate, vanilla and ice in a blender and purée till smooth.
Divide into 2 portions; top each with 1 T. whipped topping.

Nutrition Facts
Serving Size (82g)
Servings Per Container

Amount Per Serving

Calories 200   Calories from Fat 120

% Daily Value*

Total Fat 13g	**20%**
Saturated Fat 8g	**40%**
Trans Fat 0g	
Cholesterol 0mg	**0%**
Sodium 80mg	**3%**
Total Carbohydrate 23g	**8%**
Dietary Fiber 3g	**12%**
Sugars 15g	
Protein 3g	

Fruit Kanten

Makes 3-4 (1 cup) servings *Alyssa Moreau*

Kanten, aka agar-agar, marries with readily available fruit juices for a refreshing gelled dessert. Top the kanten with conventional or Greek-style yogurt, Coconut Whipped Creme (p. 38) or light whipped topping.

2 c.   apple or white grape juice
1 T.   agar-agar flakes
1-2 c.   fruit chunks of choice

Pour juice into a saucepan and sprinkle in the agar flakes. Allow the agar to soften, about 3 minutes. Bring juice to a boil, stirring to dissolve the agar. Cover, reduce heat and simmer 10 minutes. Remove from heat and let sit for about 10 minutes. Add fruit pieces and pour into a mold or 4 dessert dishes. Allow to set at room temperature. Cover with plastic wrap and chill before serving.

Variation: Try other juices, such as dark cherry or berry juices, with berries and bananas.

Nutrition Facts

Serving Size (82g)
Servings Per Container

Amount Per Serving

Calories 200	Calories from Fat 120

	% Daily Value*
Total Fat 13g	20%
Saturated Fat 8g	40%
Trans Fat 0g	
Cholesterol 0mg	0%
Sodium 80mg	3%
Total Carbohydrate 23g	8%
Dietary Fiber 3g	12%
Sugars 15g	
Protein 3g	

CHAPTER TEN

Sweet Child of Mine: Family-Friendly Treats

The key to defeating childhood obesity doesn't lie solely in dietary choices; weight gain is intimately related to family dynamics. Beyond food choices, appropriate modeling plays a strong role. And that includes cooking and eating in company with family members. Here are kid-friendly recipes to enjoy and make together.

Gingery Fruit and Nut Bars

Makes 6 bars *Alyssa Moreau*

Quinoa flakes are a great way to add a bit of protein to energy bars.

1 c.	almonds
¼ c.	pumpkin seeds
¼ c.	sunflower seeds
¼ c.	apricots, chopped
½ c.	dates, chopped
¼ c.	quinoa flakes
¼ tsp.	salt
¼ c.	apple juice
1 T.	crystallized ginger, minced (opt.)

Preheat oven to 325 degrees. Line baking sheet with parchment paper. In a food processor, coarsely chop the almonds. Add the pumpkin and sunflower seeds and pulse to partially break down seeds. Add the dates and pulse until mixture starts to stick together. Transfer to a large mixing bowl and mix in the quinoa flakes, salt and ginger. Pour apple juice over mixture and, using hands, mix well. Press into rectangular musubi molds; turn out of molds and bake for 10 minutes or until lightly browned.

Variation:
- Alternately, you can pat into a rectangle and cut into even-size bars.

Nutrition Facts

Serving Size (64g)
Servings Per Container

Amount Per Serving

Calories 270   Calories from Fat 150

	% Daily Value*
Total Fat 17g	26%
Saturated Fat 1.5g	8%
Trans Fat 0g	
Cholesterol 0mg	0%
Sodium 105mg	4%
Total Carbohydrate 24g	8%
Dietary Fiber 5g	20%
Sugars 12g	
Protein 8g	

Flax Energy Bars

Makes approximately 6 bars *Alyssa Moreau*

Many commercial energy bars may be low in fat but are packed with sugar. This version makes use of fruit, nuts and cereal for sweetness and crunch.

¼ c.	flax seeds, ground to form meal
½ c.	apple juice
1 c.	date pieces, chopped
½ c.	peanut butter
½ tsp.	vanilla
1 c.	shredded unsweetened coconut
½ c.	protein powder or dry milk powder
1 c.	crispy rice cereal (conventional or health food type)
¼ c.	chopped walnut
¼ c.	raisins or dried fruit of choice
½ tsp.	cinnamon
⅛ tsp.	salt

Place flax meal in a large mixing bowl. Pour apple juice over and add chopped dates; mix well. Let sit about 10 minutes or until mixture start to thicken. Add peanut butter and vanilla. Stir well. In a separate bowl, combine dry ingredients. Add to the thickened flax mixture and, using your hands, mix together. Spread onto parchment paper-lined sheet pan and cover with another piece of parchment. Using a rolling pin, roll to an even thickness, pushing in edges to create a rectangle form. Chill until firm. Cut into bars and individually wrap in plastic wrap (or use a musubi mold to form individual bars; then chill and wrap). Or roll into balls.

Variations:
- Substitute any other nut butter.
- Substitute granola for rice cereal.

Nutrition Facts

Serving Size (113g)
Servings Per Container

Amount Per Serving

Calories 470   Calories from Fat 260

% Daily Value*

Total Fat 29g	**45%**
Saturated Fat 13g	**65%**
Trans Fat 0g	
Cholesterol 10mg	**3%**
Sodium 230mg	**10%**
Total Carbohydrate 47g	**16%**
Dietary Fiber 7g	**28%**
Sugars 33g	
Protein 12g	

Crustless Broccoli–Cheddar Quiche

Makes 8 servings *Carol Nardello*

This tasty quiche is quick to prepare and tastes delicious whenever it is served—even at room temperature for a home lunch or a late afternoon snack. The lack of a pastry crust cuts the fat content compared to conventional quiche.

1½ T.	panko crumbs
5	eggs (or equivalent egg substitute), beaten
1 T.	vegetable oil
1½ c.	whole milk
½ c.	onion, diced
¼ tsp.	Lawry's Seasoned Salt
1 sml.	head of broccoli, chopped
⅛ tsp.	black pepper
2 c.	Cheddar cheese, grated

Preheat oven to 375 degrees. Lightly grease a 10-inch quiche pan or pie plate. Sprinkle the pan all over with panko crumbs. Heat a large skillet over medium heat. Add oil and sauté onion and broccoli together for 5 minutes or until wilted. Spread cooked vegetables in crumb-lined pan. Sprinkle with cheese. Whisk eggs, milk and seasonings together until smooth. Pour over cheese and bake in hot oven for 25 minutes or until center is set. Cool slightly before slicing.

Variation:
- Substitute ⅛ teaspoon each salt and dry mustard for the Lawry's Seasoned Salt.

Nutrition Facts

Serving Size (154g)
Servings Per Container

Amount Per Serving

Calories 160   Calories from Fat 70

	% Daily Value*
Total Fat 8g	12%
Saturated Fat 3g	15%
Trans Fat 0g	
Cholesterol 145mg	48%
Sodium 370mg	15%
Total Carbohydrate 8g	3%
Dietary Fiber 2g	8%
Sugars 3g	
Protein 14g	

Monkey Fruits

Makes 4 servings *Carol Nardello*

This recipe evolved while creating healthy food snacks for the "Cooking Up A Rainbow" program—the statewide initiative to teach healthy snack preparation as an activity for after-school programs to help prevent childhood obesity. It has become the top favorite snack of all of the children involved.

4	apple bananas, peeled and sliced into 2-inch rounds (OR 8 whole strawberries, halved)
½ c.	fat-free vanilla yogurt
4 T.	shredded coconut or crushed cereal (granola, Grape Nuts, whole grain snack puffs, etc.)

Roll banana slices or berry halves one by one in yogurt to completely coat. Place coconut or crumbs into a small cup or bowl and drop in a yogurt-covered fruit slice. Shake bowl to cover fruit with crumbs. Pierce with a toothpick and place on serving platter.

Variation:
Any bite-sized fruit chunks will do, including pineapple, pear, apple or oranges. Monkeys love them, too!

Nutrition Facts

Serving Size (143g)
Servings Per Container

Amount Per Serving

Calories 170	Calories from Fat 35
	% Daily Value*
Total Fat 4g	**6%**
Saturated Fat 3.5g	**18%**
Trans Fat 0g	
Cholesterol 0mg	**0%**
Sodium 45mg	**2%**
Total Carbohydrate 30g	**10%**
Dietary Fiber 3g	**12%**
Sugars 20g	
Protein 4g	

Awesome Cornmeal Pancakes with Sugar-Free Fruit Purée

Makes 15 pancakes   *Alyssa Moreau*

These delightfully nutty and interestingly textured pancakes make nutritious and filling snacks and an educational and enjoyable family project. Younger members of the family can help gather ingredients and tools and measure the ingredients. Older members can cook the cakes. Unlike conventional white flour pancakes, these make a nice wrap even when they're room temperature. If you're serving the pancakes hot, skip the butter and conventional syrup in favor of sliced bananas, homemade sugarless fruit purée (see below), a sprinkle of cinnamon or a smear of sugar-free preserves. For cold pancake wraps, fill with peanut butter or other nut butters, sugar-free preserves, lowfat yogurt, fat-free cream cheese, applesauce—anything spreadable and healthy—or even a slice of cheese, turkey or ham or a sandwich spread.

1 c.	boiling water
¾ c.	medium or coarse stoneground cornmeal
1 T.	agave syrup (or molasses)
1 c.	reduced-fat buttermilk*
1½ c.	whole wheat pastry flour
¾ t.	salt
3 t.	baking powder
¼ t.	baking soda
2 T.	vegetable oil (canola or safflower)
	Egg replacement equivalent to 2 eggs**

In a large mixing bowl, combine water and cornmeal, stirring until smooth and slightly thickened. Stir in agave syrup and buttermilk. In a medium bowl or an oversize (8-cup) measuring cup, whisk together the pastry flour salt, baking powder and baking soda.

Stir into cornmeal mixture, combining well. Place a large frying pan or griddle over medium heat and spray with non-stick spray or wipe lightly with an oiled paper towel. Set the oven to warm and place a heatproof platter in the oven. Stir in egg replacement and vegetable oil. Mix well. Using a ladle, pour out sufficient batter to make a medium-size pancake

Nutrition Facts

Serving Size (56g)
Servings Per Container

Amount Per Serving	
Calories 100	Calories from Fat 25
	% Daily Value*
Total Fat 3g	5%
Saturated Fat 0g	0%
Trans Fat 0g	
Cholesterol 0mg	0%
Sodium 260mg	11%
Total Carbohydrate 16g	5%
Dietary Fiber 2g	8%
Sugars 2g	
Protein 3g	

(about 4 inches across). Watch for bubbles to form, distributed throughout the pancake; turn and cook another half minute or so. Transfer pancakes to warm platter in oven.

*Or 1 c. lowfat milk mixed with 1 teaspoon vinegar; the milk will "clabber," souring and thickening slightly.

** If using Ener-G brand, use 3 t. Ener-G and 4 T. water.

Sugar-free fruit purée: In a blender or food processor purée 1 c. strawberries, chopped fresh or canned peaches or pears, sliced apple bananas or creamy-textured tropical fruit along with ¼ c. apple or orange juice. After it's puréed, you can add ¼ c. toasted nuts or dried fruit for textural interest; cinnamon or other spices or aromatics such as grated ginger to taste. Remove to a bowl; taste and sweeten to taste with Splenda, Truvia or stevia.

Fruit Smoothies

Makes 4 servings   *Carol Nardello*

Here's another goodie developed for "Cooking Up A Rainbow." As a result of this recipe for fruit smoothies, every unit trained (there are hundreds) purchased blenders so they could teach the children how to enjoy these healthy fruit snacks.

1 c.	diced fresh fruit or berries
3/4 c.	fat-free vanilla yogurt
1 c.	vanilla soy milk
6	ice cubes

Combine everything in a blender and purée until smooth. Add a dash of ground cinnamon for extra flavor and to help manage blood sugar levels.

Nutrition Facts

Serving Size (186g)
Servings Per Container

Amount Per Serving

Calories 90   Calories from Fat 10

% Daily Value*

Total Fat 1g	2%
Saturated Fat 0g	0%
Trans Fat 0g	
Cholesterol 0mg	0%
Sodium 70mg	3%
Total Carbohydrate 16g	5%
Dietary Fiber 1g	4%
Sugars 12g	
Protein 4g	

Garden Tacos

Makes 8 servings *Carol Nardello*

Here's a healthy, high-protein, low-fat snack for all ages. This recipe combines canned tuna fish with fresh-made salsa and is served in a crispy Romaine lettuce leaf. Tacos don't always have to be fried tortillas! Served chilled. Kids can help make them, and they love to eat them.

2	tomatoes, chopped
½	sweet onion, minced
½	jalapeño pepper, cored, seeded, and minced finely (optional)
1 clove	garlic, minced
	Zest and juice of ½ lime
¼ c.	cilantro, chopped (optional)
2 (6-oz.)	cans tuna packed in water, drained
8 lg.	Romaine leaves, washed and stems removed
¾ c.	Cheddar cheese, grated

Prepare salsa in a medium bowl by combining the tomatoes, onion, jalapeño, garlic, lime zest and juice. Mix well and chill until needed. Combine drained tuna fish with prepared salsa, mixing well. Spread out Romaine leaves and evenly divide filling among them. Sprinkle with cheese and serve.

Nutrition Facts

Serving Size (131g)
Servings Per Container

Amount Per Serving

Calories 90   Calories from Fat 20

	% Daily Value*
Total Fat 2g	3%
Saturated Fat 0.5g	3%
Trans Fat 0g	
Cholesterol 20mg	7%
Sodium 250mg	10%
Total Carbohydrate 5g	2%
Dietary Fiber 1g	4%
Sugars 2g	
Protein 14g	

Blueberry Slump

Makes 4 servings *Carol Nardello*

This dish was developed for a class in healthy cooking for kids—in a classroom where there was no oven. It's an old childhood favorite from New England that is cooked on the stovetop. The kids got a kick out of the name, and it was their favorite of everything we cooked in class.

¼ c.	Splenda
1 c.	water
	Juice and zest of ½ lemon
½ tsp.	cinnamon
4 c.	fresh or frozen blueberries
2 c.	flour
4 tsp.	baking powder
½ tsp.	salt
2 T.	Splenda
⅔ c.	milk

In a large, deep skillet bring Splenda, water, lemon zest and juice, and cinnamon to a boil. Add berries and return to boil. Prepare dough in a large bowl by combining flour, baking powder, salt and Splenda. Stir in milk a little at a time just until dough is moistened and sticking together. Avoid overmixing. Drop tablespoonfuls of dough into simmering fruit, reduce heat to low, cover pan and continue cooking for 8-10 minutes or until dumplings are puffed and cooked through. Serve warm.

Nutrition Facts

Serving Size (162g)
Servings Per Container

Amount Per Serving

Calories 170   Calories from Fat 10

% Daily Value*

Total Fat 1g	2%
Saturated Fat 0g	0%
Trans Fat 0g	
Cholesterol 0mg	0%
Sodium 430mg	18%
Total Carbohydrate 37g	12%
Dietary Fiber 2g	8%
Sugars 9g	
Protein 4g	

Bird's Nests

Makes 1 serving   *Carol Nardello*

Are you having trouble getting your children to eat eggs? This recipe is fun to make and healthy. Give it a try; kids like the look of the egg nesting in the bread. Salsa adds vegetables; cheese adds flavor and protein.

1	egg
1 slice	whole wheat bread
1 tsp.	vegetable oil
	Fresh Salsa (same recipe as for garden tacos, p. 135)
1 T.	Cheddar cheese, grated

Preheat griddle or small skillet over medium-low heat. Cut a round out of the center of the bread using a small cup or glass and reserve. Oil hot pan and place the bread inside. Crack an egg into the hole cut out in the bread. Cook until the white becomes opaque. Gently flip over to continue cooking to desired doneness. Toast bread cut-out on both sides in pan. Serve as toast with prepared egg. Top with salsa and grated cheese and serve.

Nutrition Facts

Serving Size (186g)
Servings Per Container

Amount Per Serving

Calories 90   Calories from Fat 10

                                                      % Daily Value*
Total Fat 1g   2%
    Saturated Fat 0g   0%
    Trans Fat 0g
Cholesterol 0mg   0%
Sodium 70mg   3%
Total Carbohydrate 16g   5%
    Dietary Fiber 1g   4%
    Sugars 12g
Protein 4g

Cranberry–Chocolate Crunch Cookies

Makes 12 servings of 2 cookies each *Sharon Kobayashi*

This cookie has it all. Coating the cookies in cornflakes instead of mixing them in with the dough gives extra crunch. Dried fruit adds sweetness and a chewy texture.

10 oz.	Oat Pie Crust (p. 111)
1 T.	sugar
2 tsp.	vanilla extract
⅓ c.	dried cranberries, about 1½ oz.
⅓ c.	semi-sweet chocolate chips, about 2 oz.
2½ c.	cornflakes, slightly crushed

Preheat oven to 350 degrees. Line a baking sheet with parchment paper or a silicon baking sheet. Prepare the pie crust recipe as directed, but add 1 T. sugar and 2 tsp. vanilla and mix in the cranberries and chocolate chips. Pour cornflakes onto a large plate. Drop heaping teaspoons into the cornflakes (do 6 cookies at a time). Use cornflakes to flip pieces of dough over to coat. Gently roll into balls and flatten, flipping over often to avoid sticking.

You should flip each cookie twice to get to ⅛-inch thickness. Place cookies on the baking sheet (evenly spaced). Bake for 30 minutes or until golden brown. Transfer to a rack to cool completely.

Variations:
- Roll cookies in Rice Krispies instead of cornflakes.
- Add ⅔ c. cranberries and omit chocolate. Roll in sesame seeds and minced nuts.
- Use ⅔ c. trail mix instead of the cranberries and chocolate.

Nutrition Facts

Serving Size (40g)
Servings Per Container

Amount Per Serving

Calories 160	Calories from Fat 45

	% Daily Value*
Total Fat 5g	8%
Saturated Fat 2g	10%
Trans Fat 0g	
Cholesterol 20mg	7%
Sodium 125mg	5%
Total Carbohydrate 24g	8%
Dietary Fiber 2g	8%
Sugars 9g	
Protein 3g	

Birdseed Bars

Makes 8 bars *Alyssa Moreau*

People used to say of someone who was chattering a lot, "Well, you've had your birdseed today!" If you serve these richly textured bar cookies, you can say that for real.

½ c.	quinoa flakes
½ c.	whole wheat pastry flour
2 T.	brown rice flour
2 T.	millet (optional)
¼ tsp.	salt
½ c.	dates, chopped (about 6 large, seeded)
½ c.	sunflower seeds
¾ c.	pumpkin seeds
¼ c.	sesame seeds
½ c.	tahini (sesame butter)
	maple syrup

Quinoa grain

Preheat oven to 350 degrees. Oil a 7-by-11-inch baking dish. Combine the first 5 ingredients in a large mixing bowl. In a food processor, pulse the dates with the sunflower, pumpkin and sesame seeds until just combined (mixture is sticky). Add to the dry mix and, using hands, mix together well. Whisk tahini and maple syrup together in another bowl. Add to seed dough and stir well to get all ingredients incorporated. Pour into prepared pan and bake about 20 minutes or until it is lightly browned on edges and top and is firm to touch. Cool and cut.

Variations:

- Substitute ¼ cup applesauce for ¼ cup of the tahini if you like a less rich cookie.
- To make the recipe gluten-free, replace whole wheat pastry flour with sorghum or millet flour and add ½ tsp. guar or xanthan gum to the dry mix.

Nutrition Facts

Serving Size (102g)
Servings Per Container

Amount Per Serving

Calories 450	Calories from Fat 220

	% Daily Value*
Total Fat 25g	38%
Saturated Fat 3.5g	18%
Trans Fat 0g	
Cholesterol 0mg	0%
Sodium 105mg	4%
Total Carbohydrate 46g	15%
Dietary Fiber 5g	20%
Sugars 20g	
Protein 16g	

Pineapple–Mango Slump

Makes 8 servings   *Carol Nardello*

Here's another version of this stovetop dessert featuring two favorite fruits.

2 c.	flour
4 tsp.	baking powder
½ tsp.	salt
2 T.	Splenda
⅔ c.	milk
1 whole	pineapple, peeled, cored, and diced
1 lg.	mango, peeled, seeded, and diced
1 T.	Splenda Brown Sugar Blend
1 c.	water
	Juice of ½ lemon
½ tsp.	cinnamon

In a large mixing bowl, combine flour, baking powder, salt and Splenda. Stir in milk a little at a time until dough sticks together. Avoid overmixing. In a large, deep skillet, bring Splenda Blend, water, lemon juice and cinnamon to a boil. Add diced fruits and bring back to the boil. Reduce heat and drop tablespoonfuls of dough into simmering fruit. Reduce heat, cover tightly and continue to cook for 8-10 minutes or until dumplings are puffed and cooked through. Serve warm.

Nutrition Facts
Serving Size (173g)
Servings Per Container

Amount Per Serving

Calories 170	Calories from Fat 10
	% Daily Value*
Total Fat 1g	2%
Saturated Fat 0g	0%
Trans Fat 0g	
Cholesterol 0mg	0%
Sodium 430mg	18%
Total Carbohydrate 38g	13%
Dietary Fiber 2g	8%
Sugars 8g	
Protein 4g	

Crispy Rice Squares

Makes 9-12 pieces *Alyssa Moreau*

Here's a different version of a familiar favorite. Find brown rice crisp cereal in health food stores. This is one kids can easily help make.

1 c.	maple syrup (the real thing, please)
1 T.	agar flakes (or arrowroot powder)
1 c.	natural peanut butter
1 tsp.	vanilla
¼ tsp.	salt
4 c.	brown rice crisp cereal

Heat maple syrup in a large pan with the agar flakes. Bring to a boil and cook to dissolve agar or arrowroot. Add peanut butter, vanilla and salt. Mix well. Remove from heat and stir in cereal. Oil or spray a 7-by-11-inch or 8-by-8-inch pan and firmly pat the mixture evenly into the pan. Chill. Cut into squares and serve.

Variations:
Add dried fruits and nuts to the mix. Substitute another nut butter (cashew, almond). Top with melted chocolate with a little almond milk and agave syrup to sweeten.

Nutrition Facts

Serving Size (59g)
Servings Per Container

Amount Per Serving

Calories 240	Calories from Fat 100
	% Daily Value*
Total Fat 11g	17%
Saturated Fat 2g	10%
Trans Fat 0g	
Cholesterol 0mg	0%
Sodium 190mg	8%
Total Carbohydrate 31g	10%
Dietary Fiber 2g	8%
Sugars 19g	
Protein 6g	

Mango–Banana–Mac Nut Granola (or Gorp)

Makes 2 cups *Alyssa Moreau*

This recipe gives you a choice of making granola to eat as cereal or on yogurt, or adding a few ingredients to create a nutrient-packed trail mix, aka "gorp" (a mixture of salty and sweet) for your next hike in the woods. There's little cooking involved, and even younger children can help with measuring and mixing. Make it a family project—and feel free to vary the ingredients, but steer clear of too many sugary ingredients.)

For the granola:

1¼ c.	regular rolled oats	3 T.	honey or agave
¼ c.	chopped macadamia nuts	1 T.	coconut oil*
2 T.	dry-roasted soy nuts	¼ c.	coconut milk or apple juice
½ tsp.	cinnamon	1 tsp.	vanilla
½ tsp.	ground ginger	½ c.	dried mango, bite-size pieces
	Pinch salt	½ c.	dried bananas, bite-size pieces

Preheat oven to 325 degrees. Line baking sheet with parchment or silicone baking liner. In a medium bowl, combine the oats, macadamia nuts, soy nuts, dry spices and salt. Mix well. In a small bowl, combine the honey, coconut oil, coconut milk and vanilla. Pour over the dry mix and combine, stirring well until evenly moistened. Spread mixture on the greased baking sheet and bake for 15 minutes. Remove from the oven and stir, breaking the large chunks into smaller pieces. Add dried mango and banana. Bake an additional 8-10 minutes or until crisp. Cool and store in an airtight container.

To make trail mix/gorp:

1	recipe granola
½ c.	raisins, cranberries or date pieces
½ c.	salted almonds, sunflower seeds or peanuts
2-4 T.	chocolate or carob chips

Combine all together in a bowl; store in airtight container. Makes 3 cups, about ½ cup per serving.

* Coconut oil can be either refined (no coconut flavor) or unrefined (coconut flavor).

Nutrition Facts

Serving Size (101g)
Servings Per Container

Amount Per Serving

Calories 390	Calories from Fat 150

	% Daily Value*
Total Fat 17g	**26%**
Saturated Fat 9g	**45%**
Trans Fat 0g	
Cholesterol 0mg	**0%**
Sodium 45mg	**2%**
Total Carbohydrate 54g	**18%**
Dietary Fiber 7g	**28%**
Sugars 30g	
Protein 7g	

Crunchy Hand Salad with Tasty Vinaigrette

Makes 12 servings *Carol Nardello*

This is the favorite vegetable recipe enjoyed by schoolchildren in the "Cooking Up A Rainbow" series. It's a great way to get kids to eat salad!

For the vinaigrette:

2 tsp.	salt
½ tsp.	black pepper
2 T.	honey
1½ T.	Dijon mustard
1 clove	garlic, finely minced (opt.)
½ c.	apple cider vinegar
⅔ c.	olive oil

For the hand salad:

1 bunch	Romaine lettuce, cleaned and dried and separated into individual leaves
¼ c.	whole-grain snack puffs or cereal, crushed

In a jar or container with a tightly fitting lid, combine vinaigrette ingredients in the order given. Secure lid and shake hard until combined and creamy smooth. Using a spoon or paint brush, lightly coat the inside of a lettuce leaf with one teaspoonful of the prepared vinaigrette. Pour off any excess. Sprinkle crumbs all over the vinaigrette-coated lettuce leaves. Enjoy right away while crumbs are still crunchy.

Nutrition Facts

Serving Size (132g)
Servings Per Container

Amount Per Serving

Calories 420   Calories from Fat 340

	% Daily Value*
Total Fat 38g	58%
Saturated Fat 5g	25%
Trans Fat 0g	
Cholesterol 0mg	0%
Sodium 1310mg	55%
Total Carbohydrate 18g	6%
Dietary Fiber 1g	4%
Sugars 10g	
Protein 1g	

SPAM™-less Musubi

Makes 6-8 servings   *Alyssa Moreau*

Musubi doesn't have to mean SPAM™. These vegetarian musubi are a healthful snack for a child's lunch pail or after school. Combine short grain and mochi rice in a ration of 4:1 and double the amount of water (for example, 1 c. brown rice plus ¼ c. brown mochi rice to 2½ c. water). Cook 40 minutes on stovetop or prepare in rice cooker.

1 tub	fresh firm tofu, drained, patted dry and sliced into ½-inch-thick slices
	Shoyu or Bragg's Liquid Aminos, to taste
	Toasted sesame oil, to taste
	Sambal oelek chili paste, to taste
4 c.	cooked brown rice/brown mochi rice combination (see above)
1 pckg.	toasted nori (crisped black seaweed)
1 lg.	ripe avocado, seeded and sliced
½ c.	gomasio (ground, toasted sesame seeds plus salt)

In a sauté pan, cook the tofu in a little shoyu or Braggs, a splash of sesame oil and chili paste to taste. Cook over medium heat until crispy. Slice nori pieces in half lengthwise. Lay musubi mold on top of nori at one edge and pack half full with rice. Top with slice of avocado, sprinkle of gomasio and seasoned piece of tofu; push down to release rice cake from musubi mold. Remove mold and roll nori around rice cake to cover. Seal with a bit of water on nori edge. Repeat 6-8 times (depending upon amount put in molds).

Nutrition Facts

Serving Size (154g)
Servings Per Container

Amount Per Serving

Calories 350   Calories from Fat 110

	% Daily Value*
Total Fat 13g	20%
Saturated Fat 1g	5%
Trans Fat 0g	
Cholesterol 0mg	0%
Sodium 60mg	3%
Total Carbohydrate 45g	15%
Dietary Fiber 4g	16%
Sugars 0g	
Protein 12g	

Fresh Fruit with Vanilla–Ginger Dip

Makes 12 servings *Carol Nardello*

Children enjoy dipping vegetables, so why not fruit? This mixture works wonderfully as a dip but also makes a good dressing for a quick fruit salad.

For the salad:
½	honeydew melon, thinly sliced
1 whole	cantaloupe, thinly sliced
¼	small watermelon, thinly sliced
2 c.	whole blueberries or halved strawberries
1	Korean pear, thinly sliced

For the dip:
2 c.	fat-free vanilla yogurt
1	lime, zested and juiced
2 tsp.	ginger, freshly grated
12	mint leaves, chopped finely

To prepare dip, in a medium bowl, combine yogurt, lime zest and juice, ginger and mint leaves. Stir well to blend and pour into small bowl to serve. Arrange sliced fruits on a platter and serve with dip.

Variation:
Cube fruits and toss together in a large bowl. Stir together dip ingredients and pour over fruit. Stir gently to combine.

Nutrition Facts
Serving Size (288g)
Servings Per Container

Amount Per Serving

Calories 130   Calories from Fat 5

	% Daily Value*
Total Fat 0g	0%
Saturated Fat 0g	0%
Trans Fat 0g	
Cholesterol 0mg	0%
Sodium 50mg	2%
Total Carbohydrate 29g	10%
Dietary Fiber 2g	8%
Sugars 24g	
Protein 4g	

Vegetables with Ginger–Garlic Hummus

Makes 12 servings   *Carol Nardello*

Here's an idea for fresh vegetables that children enjoy that was developed for the "Cooking Up A Rainbow" program. Children enjoy dipping just about anything, and hummus is a great source of low-fat protein and delicious served with fresh veggies. With a blender, this is a snap to prepare.

For the ginger–garlic hummus:
1 clove	garlic, chopped
1 (1-in.)	slice ginger, peeled and chopped
2 (15-oz.)	cans garbanzo beans, rinsed and drained
1½ tsp.	soy sauce
3 T.	rice vinegar
½	lemon, zested and juiced
½ tsp.	chili-garlic sauce (optional)
¼ tsp.	Chinese five spice
¼ c.	cilantro, chopped
1	green onion, chopped
3 T.	water

For dipping:
24	sliced cucumber rounds (approx. 2 cukes)
½	each red, yellow and green bell peppers, each cut into 8 strips
½	jicama, peeled and cut into 24 strips

Prepare hummus in a blender or food processor by combining all the dip ingredients except for the water. Add water as needed for a smooth, thick consistency. Place finished hummus in a small bowl and surround with prepared vegetables on a platter.

Nutrition Facts
Serving Size (154g)
Servings Per Container

Amount Per Serving

Calories 100   Calories from Fat 5

	% Daily Value*
Total Fat 0.5g	1%
Saturated Fat 0g	0%
Trans Fat 0g	
Cholesterol 0mg	0%
Sodium 75mg	3%
Total Carbohydrate 18g	6%
Dietary Fiber 5g	20%
Sugars 2g	
Protein 4g	

Almond Thumbprint Cookies

Makes 12 servings of 2 cookies each *Sharon Kobayashi*

Almonds add protein, vitamin E, fiber and great flavor to desserts. Almond flour is simply ground blanched almonds. You can make your own by blanching (to remove skins, see Mango Clafoutis recipe on page 161) and grinding almonds into a powder, or buy them already ground. As with most nuts, almond flour can be stored in the freezer for several months.

⅔ c.	all-purpose flour or whole wheat pastry flour
¾ c.	almond flour
3 T.	sugar
½ tsp.	baking powder
¼ tsp.	salt
1 lg.	egg or equivalent egg substitute
2 T.	canola oil
2 T.	lowfat ricotta cheese
4 tsp.	Simply Fruit blackberry jam
	(substitute any other flavor of Simply Fruit)

Preheat oven to 350 degrees. Line a baking pan with a silicon sheet or parchment paper. Combine flours, sugar, baking powder and salt. Mix. Add egg or egg substitute, oil and ricotta and mix well. Drop rounded teaspoonsful of dough onto sheet, spacing evenly. Using floured thumbs, make a well in each cookie. Add ¼ tsp. jam to each well. Bake for 25 minutes or till golden brown. Very carefully transfer to a cooling rack (jam will be very hot). Cool completely before eating.

Nutrition Facts

Serving Size (24g)
Servings Per Container

Amount Per Serving

Calories 80   Calories from Fat 35

% Daily Value*

Total Fat 4g	**6%**
Saturated Fat 0g	**0%**
Trans Fat 0g	
Cholesterol 20mg	**7%**
Sodium 85mg	**4%**
Total Carbohydrate 10g	**3%**
Dietary Fiber 0g	**0%**
Sugars 5g	
Protein 2g	

Chocolate Almond Float

Makes 8-10 servings *Sharon Kobayashi*

Gelatin is a good way to add texture to lower-fat mixtures, and in the case of this rich-tasting float, it stretches out the chocolate. Using almond milk in addition to extract is a good way to get some of the nutritional benefits of almonds, while also adding flavor.

4 tsp.	unflavored gelatin
2¼ c.	almond milk (or lowfat milk), chilled
5 T.	sugar
2 T.	unsweetened cocoa powder
¼ c.	light (NOT nonfat) cream cheese
1 tsp.	pure almond extract
1 tsp.	vanilla extract
¼ tsp.	instant coffee
¼ tsp.	cinnamon
2 c.	strawberries, quartered
2 c.	orange segments
	Juice from oranges
1 T.	mint leaves, sliced thin

In a small, heavy-bottomed pot, combine gelatin, cold milk, sugar and cocoa. Let sit 5 minutes, or until gelatin absorbs some liquid. Whisk together till there are no cocoa powder lumps. Cook over medium-high heat, stirring frequently, till mixture comes to a boil. Turn off heat; add cream cheese, stirring, until dissolved. If lumps or white spots remain, cool slightly and blend (in blender or with immersion blender). Add extracts, coffee and cinnamon and pour into a non-stick 8-by-8-inch pan. Allow to set 4 hours or until firm. Cut into 1-inch cubes and gently toss with cold fruit and mint.

Nutrition Facts

Serving Size (170g)
Servings Per Container

Amount Per Serving

Calories 110   Calories from Fat 20

	% Daily Value*
Total Fat 2.5g	4%
Saturated Fat 1g	5%
Trans Fat 0g	
Cholesterol 5mg	2%
Sodium 75mg	3%
Total Carbohydrate 20g	7%
Dietary Fiber 3g	12%
Sugars 16g	
Protein 3g	

Chocolate Mocha Milkshake

Makes 2 (8-ounce) servings *Sharon Kobayashi*

Instead of whole milk and ice cream, this shake makes use of oats, flax seed and fruit for a thicker mixture. If you don't have quick oats, soak rolled oats for 1 hour. Soaking the oats softens them, making them less "grainy." Flax seed also acts as a thickener and lends the milkshake a nutty flavor.

½ c.	lowfat milk
¼ c.	quick oats or rolled oats
1 T.	ground flax seed
1 T.	unsweetened cocoa powder
1 tsp.	honey
½ tsp.	instant coffee
1 tsp.	vanilla extract
1 lg.	apple banana, frozen
4	ice cubes
2 T.	fat-free whipped topping

In a large bowl, combine milk and oats and refrigerate 30 minutes. In a blender, combine oat–milk mixture, flax seed, cocoa powder, honey, coffee, vanilla and ice. Blend for 1-2 minutes, or until smooth. Divide into 2 portions; top each with 1 T. whipped topping.

Nutrition Facts

Serving Size (201g)
Servings Per Container

Amount Per Serving

Calories 190   Calories from Fat 30

	% Daily Value*
Total Fat 3.5g	5%
Saturated Fat 0.5g	3%
Trans Fat 0g	
Cholesterol 5mg	2%
Sodium 40mg	2%
Total Carbohydrate 34g	11%
Dietary Fiber 5g	20%
Sugars 16g	
Protein 6g	

Frozen Banana Bites

Makes 6 (5-piece) servings *Sharon Kobayashi*

This is a great recipe for even young kids to do (with supervision). Dates add richness and sweetness without adding refined sugar. They taste much like a Nutella fudgesicle and will appeal to the whole family. The unfrozen coating also makes a good dip for fresh fruit. You need toothpicks and a baking sheet that fits in your freezer, or several ice trays.

5	apple bananas, medium
6 T.	lowfat milk
¼ c.	lowfat ricotta cheese
4	medjool dates, seeded
2 tsp.	unsweetened cocoa powder
1 T.	natural peanut butter

Prepare bananas by peeling and slicing each banana into 6 pieces. Arrange banana slices in a single layer on a parchment paper-lined baking sheet or place one banana slice in each cube compartment of an ice cube tray. Push a toothpick firmly in the center of each slice and freeze solid. In a blender, purée together milk, ricotta, dates, cocoa and peanut butter until smooth (you may use an immersion blender, if you have one).

Dip each banana slice into coating, shaking off excess. Carefully place banana slices back on the pan (or in the ice cube tray) and freeze solid.

Nutrition Facts

Serving Size (143g)
Servings Per Container

Amount Per Serving

Calories 170   Calories from Fat 20

	% Daily Value*
Total Fat 2.5g	4%
Saturated Fat 1g	5%
Trans Fat 0g	
Cholesterol 5mg	2%
Sodium 45mg	2%
Total Carbohydrate 37g	12%
Dietary Fiber 4g	16%
Sugars 24g	
Protein 4g	

A Sweet Dash of Aloha

CHAPTER ELEVEN

The Outer Limits: Sophisticated and Contemporary

When it's time for something unusual or special—
a dessert that lifts a dinner party to a higher level—
here are some recipes to try.

Pine Nut and Orange Cookies

Makes 24-25 larger cookies; 32-36 smaller cookies *Wanda Adams*

These cookies, from the Portuguese tradition, are typical of southern Europe—very crisp, not overly sweet and meant to be enjoyed with a glass of liqueur or brandy. They also use cornmeal for all or part of the flour; Portuguese often bake with cornmeal. To make them gluten-free, use 3 cups masa harina, very finely ground cornmeal flour. Otherwise, use 2 cups all-purpose flour or whole wheat pastry flour and 1 cup masa harine, fine polenta or cornmeal. You do need to use real granulated sugar for the final coating.

½ c.	pine nuts	½ tsp.	cinnamon
2 c.	all-purpose flour	1 lg.	egg, beaten, OR equivalent
1 c.	masa harina, polenta or cornmeal		egg substitute (1 T. Ener-G plus
¼ c.	Splenda or sugar		1 T. water)
3 T.	finely grated orange zest	¼ c.	extra-virgin olive oil
	(from 2 oranges)	½ c.	fresh-squeezed orange juice
¼ tsp.	baking powder		Sugar for coating
¼ tsp.	kosher salt		

Preheat the oven to 350 degrees. Scatter pine nuts in a rimmed baking pan and place in preheated oven to toast, about 5 minutes (until you can smell the fragrance). Cool. In a medium bowl sift together flour, masa harina, Splenda, zest, baking powder, salt, cinnamon and pine nuts. In a small bowl, whisk egg substitute and water or egg; add oil and orange juice; whisk. Add to dry ingredients. Mix with your hands until dough is evenly moist and holds together when squeezed. (Add a few drops of water if dough won't hold together.)

Place about ¼ cup sugar on a flat plate or bowl. Pinch off a rounded tablespoonful of dough, roll and coat with sugar. (Or, for smaller, more delicate cookies, use a rounded teaspoonful of dough.) Place on a light-colored nonstick cookie sheet. Dip the bottom of a drinking glass in sugar and flatten cookie to slightly less than ¼ inch thick. Bake until tops are golden and edges brown—15-17 minutes (check at 12 minutes).

All-harina cookies are tan in color; those made with all-purpose flour are a lighter golden. Cool on the sheet for several minutes, then transfer to a rack. Bake one sheet at a time.

Nutrition Facts

Serving Size (37g)
Servings Per Container

Amount Per Serving

Calories 120   Calories from Fat 70

	% Daily Value*
Total Fat 8g	12%
Saturated Fat 1g	5%
Trans Fat 0g	
Cholesterol 0mg	0%
Sodium 50mg	2%
Total Carbohydrate 12g	4%
Dietary Fiber 1g	4%
Sugars 1g	
Protein 3g	

Olive Oil Lemon Cupcakes with Lemon–Basil Syrup

Makes 12 cakes *Alyssa Moreau*

These gluten-free sweet cakes light up the taste buds with the bright flavors of lemon and sweet basil. Brown rice powder, tapioca powder, potato starch and xanthan gum can be found in health food stores.

For the lemon–basil syrup:
1 c.	basil leaves
1 c.	water
½ c.	sugar
	Zest of 1 lemon

For the almond flour:
2 c.	brown rice flour
⅓ c.	tapioca powder
½ c.	potato starch
½ c.	almond meal (peeled, ground almonds)

For the cupcakes:
⅔ c.	Splenda
2½ tsp.	salt
½ tsp.	baking powder
½ tsp.	baking soda
½ tsp.	xanthan gum
½ c.	vanilla rice milk
¼ c.	olive oil
3 T.	Smart Balance margarine
1 tsp.	vanilla
1 tsp.	lemon extract
½	lemon, zested and juiced

Make syrup: Combine basil leaves, water, sugar and lemon zest in a small saucepan and bring to a boil. Stir until sugar dissolves, about 5 minutes. Remove from heat and cool 1 hour. Strain and discard solids. Pour into an airtight container and refrigerate. Keeps, covered and chilled, 5 days.

Make almond flour: In a large bowl, whisk together rice flour, tapioca powder and almond meal. Preheat oven to 375 degrees. In a large bowl, combine almond flour, Splenda, salt, baking powder, baking soda and xanthan gum. In a medium bowl, combine rice milk, olive oil, melted margarine, lemon juice and zest. Stir wet ingredients into dry and mix gently. Pour into a paper-lined 12-cup muffin pan. Bake in hot oven for 20-25 minutes. Drizzle syrup over hot cupcakes to soak in.

Nutrition Facts

Serving Size (81g)
Servings Per Container

Amount Per Serving

Calories 210   Calories from Fat 90

	% Daily Value*
Total Fat 10g	15%
Saturated Fat 1.5g	8%
Trans Fat 0.5g	
Cholesterol 0mg	0%
Sodium 200mg	8%
Total Carbohydrate 29g	10%
Dietary Fiber 1g	4%
Sugars 9g	
Protein 2g	

Mango Clafoutis

Makes 6 servings *Sharon Kobayashi*

Fresh seasonal fruit is the star of this classic French dessert that's somewhere between a pancake and custard. Whole almonds add richness usually supplied by butter or cream. Blanching almonds is easy and inexpensive. Boil water, add almonds and let sit for about 5 minutes. The brown skin (which has some bitterness) will easily peel off (just squeeze one end between thumb and forefinger). You can blanch, dry and freeze almonds for later use.

1 c.	lowfat milk
2 T.	sugar
¼ c.	blanched or slivered almonds
¼ tsp.	almond extract
1	egg
¼ c.	egg substitute
¼ tsp.	pumpkin pie spice
	Pinch salt
2 T.	flour
1 lg.	very ripe mango (out of season, substitute peaches, pear, plums, pitted cherries)
	Optional: raspberries or other fruit for garnish

Preheat oven to 375 degrees. In a blender, combine ¼ c. milk with sugar and almonds. Purée until fairly smooth (about 3-4 minutes). Add remaining milk, extract, egg, egg substitute, spice, salt and flour. Blend till smooth (about 2 minutes). Let sit for 10 minutes. Spray a 9-inch cake pan with cooking spray. Arrange mango on bottom. Pour batter over and add raspberries if desired. Bake for 30-40 minutes or until golden brown. Serve warm or at room temperature. Garnish as desired.

Nutrition Facts

Serving Size (108g)
Servings Per Container

Amount Per Serving

Calories 120	Calories from Fat 45

	% Daily Value*
Total Fat 5g	8%
Saturated Fat 1g	5%
Trans Fat 0g	
Cholesterol 40mg	13%
Sodium 75mg	3%
Total Carbohydrate 15g	5%
Dietary Fiber 1g	4%
Sugars 7g	
Protein 5g	

Coconut and Lemon Verbena Panna Cotta

Makes 4 (½-cup) servings　　　　　　　　　　　　　　　　　　　　　　　*Sharon Kobayashi*

This panna cotta has a delicate flavor and texture, with a surprisingly rich mouth feel. It's reminiscent of the local favorite, haupia. This version calls for lowfat milk as a foil to the fat of the coconut, and a little cornstarch to add body to the custard. Frozen coconut milk has a much fresher taste than canned and is worth seeking out. It can be found in most local grocery stores. Freeze unused portion (pre-measure ⅓-c. portions in small zippered plastic bags) for future use. A native of South America, lemon verbena (*Aloysia citrodora*) has a pleasing and potent citrus fragrance beloved of both chefs and makers of cologne and soaps. I grow my own lemon verbena; it's super easy to care for, prolific and a perennial. You can find plants at Hawai'i Farm Bureau Federation farmer's markets from Growing Creations. Nalo Farms and the Oahu Urban Garden Center sometimes carry lemon verbena as well.

1⅔ c.	lowfat milk, divided
1 tsp.	gelatin
2 T.	sugar
1 T.	cornstarch
⅓ c.	coconut milk (fresh-made or frozen)
12-15	lemon verbena leaves
	Optional: Serve topped with sliced strawberries and/or diced pineapple. Drizzle fruit with ¼ tsp. agave syrup

In a heavy-bottomed pot, combine 1⅓ c. of the milk, gelatin and sugar. Let sit 5 minutes at room temperature. Add cornstarch to remaining ⅓ c. milk, mix to combine.

Over medium-high heat, bring milk to the boil, stirring. When milk boils, drizzle in cornstarch mixture, stirring. Bring to a second boil and remove from heat. Stir in coconut milk, add lemon verbena and let sit 10 minutes. Remove lemon verbena and pour panna cotta into ½-c. ramekins or bowls.

Nutrition Facts

Serving Size (183g)
Servings Per Container

Amount Per Serving

Calories 270　　　Calories from Fat 80

	% Daily Value*
Total Fat 9g	14%
Saturated Fat 8g	40%
Trans Fat 0g	
Cholesterol 5mg	2%
Sodium 65mg	3%
Total Carbohydrate 42g	14%
Dietary Fiber 1g	4%
Sugars 9g	
Protein 5g	

Hawaiian Vanilla Bean and Pear Soup

Makes 4-6 servings   *Sharon Kobayashi*

Easy, unusual and elegant, this is a perfect light ending on a chilly night. Like mulled wine, the fragrant spices waft out of the bowl. The quality of the vanilla bean does most of the work. Good vanilla beans have a strong, complex aroma (floral, spicy and woody), and are soft and pliable rather than hard. Hawaiian vanilla can sometimes be found at the KCC farmer's market, at Whole Foods or online at www.hawaiianvanilla.com. Tahitian vanilla is available at specialty gourmet stores like R. Field Wine Co. Vanilla is expensive, but you can reuse the outer bean. Rinse and dry, then grind it up to make vanilla powder to use in baking, or save up 3-4 used beans to make this recipe again. Serve this soup in a Chinese soup bowl with chopsticks. A touch of sherry at the end reinforces the vanilla and adds a warming finish.

2 oz.	mung bean threads (long rice)
1	vanilla bean, Hawaiian (or other large, soft fragrant bean, like Tahitian)
1 c.	unsweetened apple juice (100-percent juice)
1 c.	Riesling wine
4 c.	water
1	whole clove
2	Bartlett pears, cored and sliced
6 T.	sugar
	Optional garnish: toasted sliced almonds and dash (½ to 1 tsp.) of good dry sherry

Soak long rice in hot water till softened (10 minutes); drain and cut into smaller pieces. Slice vanilla bean down 1 side and scrape the insides into a heavy-bottomed pot; throw in bean. Add remaining ingredients, except bean threads. Bring to a simmer and cook for 30 minutes, or until pears are tender. Add mung bean threads and cook for another 5 minutes. Serve hot, or refrigerate and serve cold. Remove vanilla bean and clove before serving. If using, garnish each portion with a sprinkle of almonds. Offer the sherry at the table.

Nutrition Facts

Serving Size (238g)
Servings Per Container

Amount Per Serving

Calories 130   Calories from Fat 0

% Daily Value*

Total Fat 0g	0%
Saturated Fat 0g	0%
Trans Fat 0g	
Cholesterol 0mg	0%
Sodium 5mg	0%
Total Carbohydrate 27g	9%
Dietary Fiber 2g	8%
Sugars 17g	
Protein 0g	

Key Lime–Avocado Pie

Makes 6-8 servings   *Alyssa Moreau*

This is a great way to use up extra avocados and a unique way to serve a favorite dessert in the Islands. The avocados, preferably local and a variety with smooth texture and no strings, should be good and ripe. The key is to taste not avocado but the tart lime paired with the light sweetness of agave. The avocado and coconut oil add good fats to this dish and wonderful texture. The pie must be chilled in order to set it up, so give yourself ample time to prepare this one. You will need to zest limes, then juice them and divide juice for use in separate parts of the recipe.

For the crust:
- ¾ c.   shredded unsweetened coconut
- ¼ c.   unsalted macadamia nuts
- ½ tsp.   lime zest
- ⅛ tsp.   salt
- 1 tsp.   lime juice
- ½ c.   dates, chopped
- 2 T.   shredded coconut

For the filling:
- 1½ c.   ripe avocado
- ⅓–½ c.   fresh lime juice
- ⅓–½ c.   agave or honey
- 4 T.   refined* coconut oil
- ¼ tsp.   salt
- Zest of ½ lime (for garnish)
- 2-3   lime slices for decoration

To make the crust: In a food processor, combine the coconuts, nuts, zest and salt and chop coarsely. Add lime juice and dates and process until it sticks together. Sprinkle a 9-inch pie plate with the remaining coconut and pat the crust on top and up the sides of the plate. Chill while making filling.

To make filling: Combine all ingredients in a blender (start with the smaller amount of lime and agave, as some avocados are wetter than others and milder in flavor; add more if needed). Blend until smooth. Adjust flavors to taste. Pour over crust and chill 4-6 hours or overnight. Garnish with remaining zest and some lime slices, if desired.

* If you use unrefined, it will add a coconut flavor to the dessert, a nice alternative if you want it to taste more tropical. Refined coconut oil is available in health food stores.

Nutrition Facts

Serving Size (83g)
Servings Per Container

Amount Per Serving

Calories 280   Calories from Fat 180

	% Daily Value*
Total Fat 21g	32%
Saturated Fat 13g	65%
Trans Fat 0g	
Cholesterol 0mg	0%
Sodium 115mg	5%
Total Carbohydrate 25g	8%
Dietary Fiber 4g	16%
Sugars 19g	
Protein 2g	

Orange–Couscous Cake

Makes 12 servings *Sharon Kobayashi*

This is a unique and impressive special-occasion cake, somewhere between orange chiffon and bread pudding. Couscous holds the flavors and keeps the cake moist, while the egg whites keep it light. Fresh oranges add even more moisture and flavor. Use sweet, local oranges when available. Select fruit that feel heavy for its size. If your oranges are not sweet enough, you may need to add a tablespoon of honey to the fruit. Serve at room temperature. If you must refrigerate the cake, cover with a damp paper towel and microwave for a few seconds before serving. Orange flower water is available at Down to Earth, Mediterranean food stores (such as the Olive Tree Café near Kahala Mall), online spice sources and some kitchen supply stores. Whole-wheat couscous can be found at natural food stores and near the rice section of some grocery stores.

1 c.	water	8	egg whites
2 T.	unsalted butter	⅓ c.	sugar
¼ tsp.	salt	½ c.	all-purpose flour
¼ c.	orange juice concentrate (frozen)	¼ c.	pistachio nuts, 1 oz. minced (or substitute almonds)
1 T.	orange zest (or zest of 2 oranges)	2	sweet, local oranges
½ tsp.	pumpkin pie spice		Optional: ½ c. Greek yogurt to top cake, offered at the table.
2 T.	honey		
½ c.	whole wheat couscous		
2 T.	orange flower water		

Bring water, butter, salt, orange concentrate, zest, spice and honey to a boil, turn off heat. Add couscous and orange flower water, let sit till it's cool and most of the liquid is absorbed. Preheat the oven to 350 degrees. Beat egg whites and sugar to soft peaks; add flour a little at a time while beating. Add ¼ of whites to couscous, and mix (to lighten). Very gently, fold couscous into remaining whites. Pour batter into an ungreased pan (with removable bottom), and sprinkle with nuts. Bake for 40 minutes, or till golden brown. Remove from the oven and immediately turn cake upside down. Cool completely before turning cake right side up. Run a butter knife around edges of cake pan, remove side and run knife around bottom. Cut the peel and white pith from oranges. Over a bowl, cut fruit away from tough dividing membranes. Squeeze juices from membrane into bowl, and discard membrane. Serve slices topped with some of the orange and juices.

Nutrition Facts

Serving Size (170g)
Servings Per Container

Amount Per Serving

Calories 160   Calories from Fat 30

% Daily Value*

Total Fat 3.5g	**5%**
Saturated Fat 1.5g	**8%**
Trans Fat 0g	
Cholesterol 5mg	**2%**
Sodium 220mg	**9%**
Total Carbohydrate 20g	**7%**
Dietary Fiber 2g	**8%**
Sugars 12g	
Protein 13g	

Thai-Infused Tapioca Pudding with Spiced Mangoes

Makes 6 servings *Carol Nardello*

This sophisticated dish is a far cry from homey, comfort-food puddings, redolent as it is of Southeast Asian aromatics. Serve it warm for more intense flavor or cover and chill before serving.

1	piece ginger (2-by-2-inch), peeled and sliced
12	Thai basil leaves
4	kaffir lime leaves (or zest of 1 lime)
3 T.	sliced lemongrass
2 c.	water
2 c.	whole milk
½ c.	sugar or Splenda
¼ tsp.	salt
½ c.	minute tapioca
1 can	unsweetened coconut milk (13.5-14-oz.)
1 lg.	mango, seeded, peeled and cubed
1 T.	fresh lime juice
	Pinch of cayenne pepper
	Thai basil sprigs

Combine ginger, basil, kaffir lime and lemongrass in food processor; process for 20 seconds. Transfer to a medium saucepan. Add 2 c. water and bring to a boil. Remove from heat and steep, uncovered, for 20 minutes. Strain mixture into a large, heavy-bottomed saucepan. Press on solids to release all of the infused liquid. Discard solids. Add milk, sugar, salt and quick-cooking tapioca. Stir well and steep for 5 minutes. Bring to a boil and reduce heat to medium to simmer for about 35 minutes, stirring frequently until mixture thickens and reduces to 2¼ cups. Stir in coconut milk. Pudding will be thin. Toss mango cubes, lime juice and cayenne to taste in a medium bowl. Divide tapioca into 6 stemmed glasses or bowls. Top with spiced mangoes; garnish with Thai basil sprigs.

Nutrition Facts

Serving Size (296g)
Servings Per Container

Amount Per Serving

Calories 310	Calories from Fat 180
	% Daily Value*
Total Fat 20g	31%
Saturated Fat 16g	80%
Trans Fat 0g	
Cholesterol 10mg	3%
Sodium 140mg	6%
Total Carbohydrate 35g	12%
Dietary Fiber 2g	8%
Sugars 19g	
Protein 4g	

Pumpkin Flan

Makes 6 servings *Sharon Kobayashi*

The lack of a crust makes this a leaner but more elegant version of pumpkin pie. If you miss the crunch, serve the flan with an amaretti (found at gourmet food stores, such as R. Field Wine Co.) or thin, crisp gingersnap cookies.

⅔ c.	sugar
12-24	pecan halves, toasted (optional)
4	eggs
½ c.	egg substitute
⅔ c.	pumpkin (canned or roasted and mashed fresh)
⅓ c.	lowfat milk
⅓ c.	lowfat cottage cheese
1 T.	vanilla
½ tsp.	pumpkin pie spice
1 T.	dark rum (optional)

Preheat oven to 325 degrees. Bring a pot of water to a simmer. Have a deep-dish pie pan or casserole dish with a 6½- to 7-inch diameter bottom ready. In a small, heavy-bottomed pan, melt ⅓ c. sugar over medium heat. Gently swirling pan to evenly cook sugar, bring the mixture to a caramel brown color. Carefully pour into pie pan or shallow casserole dish and quickly swirl caramel to cover bottom (pan will be hot; wear oven mits). If sugar sets too fast, briefly place on a burner set to low. If using pecans, place them upside-down on the caramel before it sets. Set pan aside until cool. Combine remaining sugar, eggs, pumpkin, milk, cheese, vanilla and spice in a blender. Purée until smooth. Pour over caramel; place in a larger pan, then place the pan in the oven.

Pour the hot water into larger pan to come one-third up the side of the pie pan. Cook for approximately 45 min., or until a toothpick emerges clean. Cool on the counter; cover and refrigerate at least 24 hours (up to 48 hours). Right before serving, run a butter knife around edge of pan. Place a serving platter or flat cake plate on top of the pie pan or casserole; grasp both firmly with both hands and invert, allowing flan to release onto platter. Top with 1 T. dark rum, if desired.

Nutrition Facts

Serving Size (296g)
Servings Per Container

Amount Per Serving

Calories 310	Calories from Fat 180

	% Daily Value*
Total Fat 20g	31%
Saturated Fat 16g	80%
Trans Fat 0g	
Cholesterol 10mg	3%
Sodium 140mg	6%
Total Carbohydrate 35g	12%
Dietary Fiber 2g	8%
Sugars 19g	
Protein 4g	

Hawai'i Fruits Seasonality Chart

M - Indicates MODERATE availability • **P** - Indicates PEAK availability

	JAN	FEB	MAR	APR	MAY	JUN	JUL	AUG	SEP	OCT	NOV	DEC
Atemoya	M	M						M	M	P	P	P
Avocado	P	P	M	M					M	M	P	P
Banana	M	M	M	M	M	P	P	P	P	P	M	M
Cantaloupe					M	P	P	P	M			
Honeydew					M	P	P	P	P			
Lime	P	P	P			P	P	P	P	P	P	P
Longan	M	M	M	M	M	M	M	P	P	P	M	M
Lychee	M	M	M	M	P	P	P	P	P	M	M	M
Mango			P	P	P	P	P	P	P	P	P	
Orange	P	P	P	P	M	M	M	M	P	P	P	P
Papaya	M	M	P	P	P	P	P	P	P	P	P	M
Persimmon										P	P	M
Pineapple	M	M	M	P	P	P	P	P	P	M	M	M
Rambutan	P	P	P							P	P	P
Strawberry	P	P	P	P	M	M	M			M	M	M
Starfruit	M	M	M	M					M	M	M	M
Tangerine	P	M								M	P	P
Watermelon					M	P	P	P	P	M		

Source: Hawai'i Agriculture & Food Products Directory • www.Hawaiiag.org/hdoa/

These charts were developed by the College of Tropical Agriculture and Human Resources at the University of Hawai'i in collaboration with the Hawai'i Department of Agriculture and the Hawai'i Farm Bureau Federation.

Hawai'i Vegetables Seasonality Chart

M - Indicates MODERATE availability • **P** - Indicates PEAK availability

	JAN	FEB	MAR	APR	MAY	JUN	JUL	AUG	SEP	OCT	NOV	DEC
Beans	M	M	M	P	P	P	P	P	M	M	M	M
Bittermelon	M	P	P	P	P	P	M	M				
Burdock	M	M	M				M	P	P	P	P	P
Cabbage, Chinese	P	P	P	P	P	P	P	P	M	M	M	M
Cabbage, Head	M	P	P	P	P	P	M	M	M	M	M	M
Cabbage, Asian	M	M	M				M	P	P	P	P	P
Celery		M	M	P	P	P	P	P	M	M		
Corn, Sweet	M	P	P	P	P	P	M	M	M	M	P	P
Cucumber	M	M	M	P	P	P	P	P	M	M	M	M
Daikon	M	M	M	M	M	M	P	P	P	P	P	M
Eggplant	M	P	P	P	P	P	P	M	M	M	M	M
Ginger Root		M	M	P	P	P	P	P	M	M	M	
Heart of Palm	P	P	P	P	P	P	P	P	P	P	P	P
Herbs	M	M	M	M	M	M	M	M	M	M	M	M
Lettuce, Baby Greens	M	M	M			M	M	P	P	P	P	P
Lettuce, Romaine	M	M	M	M	M	P	P	P	P	M	M	M
Lettuce, Leaf	M	M	P	P	P	P	P	M	M	M	M	M
Lū'au (Taro) Leaf				M	M	P	P	P	M	M		
Mushrooms	P	P	P	P	P	P	P	P	P	P	P	P
Onion, Round			M	P	P	P	P	P	P	M		
Onion, Green	M	M	M	M	M	M	P	P	P	P	M	M
Parsley, American	M	M	P	P	P	P	M	M				
Pepper, Green	M	M	M	P	P	P	P	P	M	M	M	M
Potato, Sweet	M	P	P	P	P	P	M	M				
Pumpkin	M		M			M	M	P	P	P	P	P
Sprouts	P	P	P	P	P	P	P	P	P	P	P	P
Squash				M	M	P	P	P	P	M	M	
Taro	M	M	P	P	P	P	P	M	M	M	P	P
Tomato	M	M	P	P	P	P	P	P	P	P	M	M
Zucchini	M	M	M			M	M	P	P	P	P	P

Source: Hawai'i Agriculture & Food Products Directory • www.Hawaiiag.org/hdoa/

Nutritional Facts for Raw Fruits

Raw Fruits	Serving Size of Edible Portion (gram weight/ounce weight)	Calories	Calories from Fat	Total Fat		Sodium	
				g	(%)	mg	(%)
Apple	1 medium (154 g/5.5 oz)	80	0	0	0	0	0
Avocado	California 1/5 medium (30 g/1.1 oz)	55	45	5	8	0	0
Banana	1 medium (126 g/4.5 oz)	110	0	0	0	0	0
Cantaloupe	1/4 medium (134 g/4.8 oz)	50	0	0	0	25	1
Grapefruit	1/2 medium (154 g/5.5 oz)	60	0	0	0	0	0
Grapes	3/4 cup (126 g/4.5 oz)	90	0	0	0	0	0
Honeydew Melon	1/10 medium (134 g/4.8 oz)	50	0	0	0	35	1
Kiwifruit	2 medium (148 g/5.3 oz)	100	10	1	2	0	0
Lemon	1 medium (58 g/2.1 oz)	15	0	0	0	5	0
Lime	1 medium (67 g/2.4 oz)	20	0	0	0	0	0
Nectarine	1 medium (140 g/5.0 oz)	70	0	0	0	0	0
Orange	1 medium (154g/5.5 oz)	70	0	0	0	0	0
Peach	1 medium (98 g/3.5 oz)	40	0	0	0	0	0
Pear	1 medium (166 g/5.9 oz)	100	10	1	2	0	0
Pineapple	2 slices; 3" diameter (112 g/4.0 oz)	60	0	0	0	10	0
Plums	2 medium (132 g/4.07 oz)	80	10	1	2	0	0
Strawberries	8 medium (147 g/5.3 oz)	45	0	0	0	0	0
Sweet Cherries	21 cherries; 1 cup (140 g/5.0 oz)	90	0	0	0	0	0
Tangerine	1 medium (109 g/3.9 oz)	50	0	0	0	0	0
Watermelon	1/8 medium melon; 2 cups diced pieces (280 g/10.0 oz)	80	0	0	0	10	0

Potassium		Total Carb		Dietary Fiber		Sugars	Protein	Vitamin A	Vitamin C	Calcium	Iron
mg	(%)	g	(%)	g	(%)	g	g	(%)	(%)	(%)	(%)
170	5	22	7	5	20	16	0	2	8	0	2
170	5	3	1	3	12	0	1	0	4	0	0
400	11	29	10	4	16	21	1	0	15	0	2
280	8	12	4	1	4	11	1	100	80	2	2
230	7	16	5	6	24	10	1	15	110	2	0
240	7	23	8	1	4	23	1	2	25	2	0
310	9	13	4	1	4	12	1	2	45	0	2
480	14	24	8	4	16	16	2	2	240	6	4
90	3	5	2	1	4	1	0	0	40	2	0
75	2	7	2	2	8	0	0	0	35	0	0
300	8	16	5	2	8	12	1	4	15	0	2
260	7	21	7	7	28	14	1	2	130	6	2
190	5	10	3	2	8	9	1	2	10	0	2
210	6	25	8	4	16	17	1	0	10	2	0
115	3	16	5	1	4	13	1	0	25	2	2
220	6	19	6	2	8	10	1	6	20	0	0
270	8	12	4	4	16	8	1	0	160	2	4
300	9	22	7	3	12	19	2	2	15	2	2
180	5	15	5	3	12	12	1	0	50	4	0
230	7	27	9	2	8	25	1	20	25	2	4

This chart was developed by the College of Tropical Agriculture and Human Resources at the University of Hawai'i in collaboration with the Hawai'i Department of Health and the Hawai'i Food Industry Association.

Nutritional Facts for Raw Fruits

Nutritional Facts for Raw Vegetables

Raw Vegetables	Serving Size of Edible Portion (gram weight/ounce weight)	Calories	Calories from Fat	Total Fat		Sodium	
				g	(%)	mg	(%)
Asparagus	5 spears (93 g/3.3 oz)	25	0	0	0	0	0
Bell Pepper	1 medium (48 g/5.3 oz)	30	0	0	0	0	0
Broccoli	1 medium stalk (148 g/5.3 oz)	45	0	0.5	1	55	2
Carrot	1 carrot; 7" long; 1/4" diameter (78 g/2.8 oz)	35	0	0	0	40	2
Cauliflower	1/6 medium head (99 g/3.5 oz)	25	0	0	0	30	1
Celery	2 medium stalks (110 g/3.9 oz)	20	0	0	0	100	4
Cucumber	1/3 medium (99 g/3.5 oz)	15	0	0	0	0	0
Green (Snap) Beans	3/4 cup cut (83 g/3.0 oz)	25	0	0	0	0	0
Green Cabbage	1/12 medium head (84 g/3.0 oz)	25	0	0	0	20	1
Green Onion	1/4 cup chopped (25 g/0.9 oz)	10	0	0	0	5	0
Iceberg Lettuce	1/6 medium head (89 g/3.2 oz)	15	0	0	0	10	0
Leaf Lettuce	1 1/2 cups shredded (85g/3.0 oz)	15	0	0	0	30	1
Mushroom	5 medium (84 g/3.0 oz)	20	0	0	0	0	0
Onion	1 medium (148 g/5.3 oz)	60	0	0	0	5	0
Potato	1 medium (148 g/5.3 oz)	100	0	0	0	0	0
Radish	7 radishes (85 g/3.0 oz)	15	0	0	0	25	1
Summer Squash	1/2 medium (98 g/3.5 oz)	20	0	0	0	0	0
Sweet Corn	kernals from 1 medium ear (90 g/3.2 oz)	80	10	1	2	0	0
Sweet Potato	1 medium; 5" long; 2" diameter (130 g/4.6 oz)	130	0	0	0	45	2
Tomato	1 medium (148 g/5.3 oz)	35	0	0.5	1	5	0

Potassium		Total Carb		Dietary Fiber		Sugars	Protein	Vitamin A	Vitamin C	Calcium	Iron
mg	(%)	g	(%)	g	(%)	g	g	(%)	(%)	(%)	(%)
230	7	4	1	2	8	2	2	10	15	2	2
270	8	7	2	2	8	4	1	8	190	2	2
540	15	8	3	5	20	3	5	15	220	6	6
280	8	8	3	2	8	5	1	270	10	2	0
270	8	5	2	2	8	2	2	0	100	2	2
350	10	5	2	2	8	0	1	2	15	4	2
170	5	3	1	1	4	2	1	4	10	2	2
200	6	5	2	3	12	2	1	4	10	4	2
190	5	5	2	2	8	3	1	0	70	4	2
70	2	2	1	1	4	1	0	2	8	0	0
120	3	3	1	1	4	2	1	4	6	2	2
230	7	4	1	2	8	2	1	40	6	4	0
300	9	3	1	1	4	0	3	0	2	0	2
240	7	14	5	3	12	9	2	0	20	4	2
720	21	26	9	3	12	3	4	0	45	2	6
230	7	3	1	0	0	2	1	0	30	2	0
260	7	4	1	2	8	2	1	6	30	2	2
240	7	18	6	3	12	5	3	2	10	0	2
350	10	33	11	4	16	7	2	440	30	2	2
360	10	7	2	1	4	4	1	20	40	2	2

Nutritional Facts for Raw Vegetables

CONTRIBUTORS

Wanda A. Adams, writer and editor

Wanda Adams was born and raised on Maui and has been a food writer in the Seattle area and in Honolulu for more than 35 years. She served the *Honolulu Advertiser* as features editor for 11 years and as food editor for another 10 before the newspaper's closure in 2010. She is the author of The Island Plate: 150 Years of Recipes and Food Lore from *The Honolulu Advertiser* (Island Heritage, 2005), which has sold 30,000 copies, as well as *The Island Plate II* and *Entertaining Island Style.* She has contributed to the culinary Web site ShareYourTable.com and operates a Web site and blog at ourislandplate.com. She is a freelance food writer and editor, working from her home in Kapālama on the island of Oʻahu, where she lives with her husband and two cats.

Adriana Torres Chong, food photographer

Adriana Torres Chong was born in Mexico City and has worked in Mexico, France and the U.S. She holds a bachelor's degree in gastronomy from the Universidad del Claustro de Sor Juana in Mexico City. She has worked at several highly acclaimed restaurants, including Au Pied de Cochon in Paris, and also worked as head chef at Tefal-Krups-Moulinex Center, a training center showcasing a variety of kitchenware. Chong lives in Honolulu where she combines her two passions, free-lancing as a food stylist and photographer and teaching Mexican cuisine at the University of Hawaiʻi's Culinary Institute of the Pacific at Kapiʻolani Community College. Her past clients include the Kāhala Mandarin Oriental, Halekulani and the Kāhala Hotel and Resort. This book is her seventh cookbook collaboration with Watermark Publishing since 2007.

Frank Gonzales, editor
Non-Credit Culinary Arts Program Coordinator
Kapiʻolani Community College (KCC), University of Hawaiʻi (UH)

Frank Gonzales is a graduate of Stanford University with a bachelor's degree in International Relations and is a National Hispanic Merit Scholar. He also holds Associate of Science degrees in Culinary Arts and Patisserie. His responsibilities at KCC include designing and implementing public and contract culinary education and training programs. Prior to arriving in Hawaiʻi in 2001, he lived and worked in California's Silicon Valley as an account executive, first with Cunningham Communications and then with Blanc & Otus Public Relations. He worked with clients ranging from high tech start-up companies to Hewlett-Packard. He has also been a research analyst at the Business Intelligence Center of SRI International in Menlo Park, California, and spent several years in Washington, D.C., as a political analyst.

Grant Itomitsu, contributing author and editor
Registered Dietitian and instructor
Kapiʻolani Community College (KCC), University of Hawaiʻi (UH).

Grant Itomitsu holds a Bachelor of Science degree in the field of Food Science and Human Nutrition from UH. He has vast experience working as a clinical dietitian and educator in multiple facilities, including Kamehameha Schools, Kuakini Medical Center, St. Francis Medical Center, St. Francis Homecare, Straub Hospital, Hale Nani and Avalon Nursing facilities. Through working in multiple areas of nutrition, such as food service, clinical nutrition and education, he has gained personal insight and unique perspective in Hawaiʻi's diverse population. He adheres to the principle that diets are not temporary quick fixes but a perpetual investment in safeguarding a person's quality of life.

Sharon Kobayashi, contributing chef author
Chef owner
Latitude 22, LLC

Sharon Kobayashi holds a bachelor's degree in Zoology and a master's degree in Evolutionary Ecology and Conservation Biology from the University of Hawai'i. She also studied biology at the University of Washington and Cornell University, and was a biologist for the federal government. Sharon has an associate's degree in Culinary Arts from the Culinary Institute of the Pacific at Kapi'olani Community College. She has worked in restaurants in Hawai'i, Washington and California. Her professional culinary experience includes French, Pacific Rim, Japanese fusion, vegan and raw foods. She translates her eclectic experiences and interests in nutrition science and the culinary arts into product development for her business, Latitude 22. Latitude 22, dba Akamai Foods, specializes in global cuisine with a healthy flair. Their signature product, low-fat oatcakes, can be found in stores throughout Hawai'i.

Daniel Leung, contributing author and editor
Educational Specialist
Culinary Institute of the Pacific at Kapi'olani Community College (KCC), University of Hawai'i (UH).

Daniel Leung holds a master's degree in Social Work from UH and an associate's degree in Culinary Arts from KCC. He is an alumnus of the East West Center's Institute of Culture and Communication. His responsibilities at KCC include coordinating agritourism programs, health and wellness culinary education programs and international culinary education tours. He is also an instructor for Chinese cuisine classes for the continuing education programs. Leung was a program administrator in human services for 15 years, with experience in program development and management of cross-cultural and international programs in Australia, Hong Kong and Hawai'i.

Alyssa Moreau, contributing chef author
Chef owner
Divine Creations

Alyssa Moreau has been a personal chef for private households since 2000, focusing on healthy vegetarian meals. Prior to that she worked with naturopathic physician Dr. Laurie Steelsmith as a dietary counselor for patients with various health challenges such as food allergies, diabetes, heart disease, cancer and weight loss/gain. She also worked with a computer-assisted analysis program monitoring personal diets. Graduating from the University of Hawaiʻi with B.A. in Environmental Health, she worked in the local restaurant industry for over 15 years. Moreau offers private cooking lessons and caters for small parties. She has conducted cooking demonstrations for the Vegetarian Society as well as other private organizations. She has taught Vegetarian/Wellness Cooking Classes for the continuing education programs at KCC since 2002.

Carol Nardello, contributing chef author

Carol Nardello is a certified executive chef and chef instructor at the Culinary Institute of the Pacific, Kapiʻolani Community College. Her course specialties are Gluten-Free Cooking, Easy Entertaining, and Healthy Cooking and Nutrition for Families. She is also a nutrition specialist trainer for after-school programs on Oʻahu including Fun 5, A+, Kamaʻaina Kids, the Department of Education and the YMCA. She was formerly executive chef at the Sub-Zero/Wolf Honolulu showroom, where she coordinated culinary classes, cooking demonstrations and product sales until the showroom closed. A mother of three, she feels strongly about teaching healthy foods and nutrition to other families.

Ronald K. Takahashi, M.B.A., CHE, CFBE, principal investigator, editor
Culinary Arts Department Chairperson
Culinary Institute of the Pacific at Kapi'olani Community College (KCC), University of Hawai'i (UH).

Ronald Takahashi is a tenured associate professor and department chair at KCC. He has a total of more than 40 years of professional and academic experience in the business aspects of both the culinary and hospitality industries. His professional experience includes having owned and/or operated a wide range of food and beverage operations for both hotels and independent restaurants, located in Hawai'i and California. He has also been entrepreneur in the visitor industry, having initiated a new concept in water sports activities on O'ahu. Along with teaching courses in Hospitality Purchasing & Cost Control, he has also taught classes in Dining Room Service, Food Service Supervision, Menu Merchandising, Equipment Layout and Design and the Hospitality Industry.

INDEX

A

AGAR-AGAR (Kanten)
    About, 16
    Coffee "Jell-O" with Coconut Whipped Creme, 38
    Fruit Kanten, 123
Agave syrup, about, 24
ALMONDS
    Almond butter, in Bliss Balls, 29
    Almond flour mix, 76, 82, 160
    Almond meal, 76
    Almond milk, about, 16
    Almond Panna Cotta with Tropical Fruit Confetti, 28
    Almond Thumbprint Cookies, 151
    Blanched, in Mango Clafoutis, 161
    Chocolate Almond Float, 152
Anadama Bread, Gluten-Free, 77
APPLES
    Applesauce, as egg substitute, 47
    Applesauce, as sugar substitute, 14, 24
    Healthy Applesauce Spice Cake, 107
    Quick Apple–Date Sticky Buns, 67
    Tarte Tatin, 115
Apple bananas, see BANANAS
AVOCADO
    Chocolate Pudding Pie, 36
    Key Lime–Avocado Pie, 166
    Melon and Mint Sorbet, 120
    SPAM™-less Musubi, 146
Awesome Cornmeal Pancakes, 132
AZUKI BEANS
    About, 16
    Azuki Bean Mochi Cake, 40

B

Baked Doughnuts, 37
BANANAS
    As egg substitute, 47
    As sugar substitute, 24
    Banana–Mango–Macadamia Nut Muffins, 68
    Frozen Banana Bites, 154
    Gluten-Free Banana Bread, 85
    Mango–Banana–Mac Nut Granola or Gorp, 144
    Monkey Fruits, 130
    Sugar-Free Banana Snack Cake, 43
Barley malt, about, 24
BEANS
    Azuki Bean Mochi Cake, 40
    Bean flours, 76
    Bean thread (long rice), in Hawaiian Vanilla Bean and Pear Soup, 165
    Garbanzo, in Eggnog Pudding, 53
    Garbanzo, in Gluten-Free Chocolate Spice Cake, 87
    Garbanzo, in Vegetables with Ginger–Garlic Hummus, 149
Bird's Nests (egg-and-toast snacks), 139
Birdseed Bars, 141
BISCUITS
    Oat Biscuits, 69
    Sesame Biscuits, 72
Black Fruit Tart, 110
BLACKBERRIES
    Black Fruit Tart, 110
Bliss Balls, 29
BLUEBERRIES
    Blueberry and Lemon Cobbler, 112
    Blueberry Sauce, with Gluten-Free Pancakes, 97
    Blueberry Slump, 136
BREADS
    Gluten-Free Anadama Bread, 77
    Gluten-Free Banana Bread, 85
    Gluten-Free Cornbread, 80
    Gluten-Free Mango Bread, 84
    Herb Braided Bread, 62
    Honey Whole Wheat Dough, 59

Magical Bread (GF), 79
Near East Manapua, 64
Strawberry Ricotta Pizza, 60
Whole Wheat Rolls, 61
Brown rice syrup, about, 24

C

CAKES
Azuki Bean Mochi Cake, 40
Carrot and Spice Cupcakes with Pineapple–Cream Cheese Frosting, 101
Chocolate Beet Cake with Chocolate Glaze, 102
Easy Lemon Tiramisu (GF), 100
Gluten-Free Carrot Cake, 88
Gluten-Free Chocolate Pudding Cake, 89
Gluten-Free Chocolate Spice Cake, 87
Gluten-Free Pumpkin Spice Cupcakes with Cream Cheese–Maple Icing, 82
Healthy Applesauce–Spice Cake, 107
No-Bake Cheesecake, 105
Olive Oil Lemon Cupcakes with Lemon–Basil Syrup, 160
Orange Couscous Cake, 169
Sugar-Free Banana Snack Cake, 43
Strawberry Gelatin Cake, 104
Strawberry Shortcake, with Oat Biscuits, 69

CARROT
Carrot and Spice Cupcakes with Pineapple–Cream Cheese Frosting, 101
Gluten-Free Carrot Cake, 88

CHOCOLATE
Chocolate Almond Float, 152
Chocolate Beet Cake with Chocolate Glaze, 102
Chocolate Glaze, with Chocolate Beet Cake, 102
Chocolate-Dipped Macaroons, 26
Chocolate Mocha Milkshake, 153
Chocolate Pudding Pie, 36
Cranberry–Chocolate Crunch Cookies, 140
Gluten-Free Chocolate Pudding Cake, 89
Gluten-Free Chocolate Spice Cake, 87
Peppermint–Chocolate Chip Cookies, 49
Ultimate Chocolate Supreme Cookies, 95

Clafoutis, Mango, 161

COCONUT
Chocolate-Dipped Macaroons, 26
Coconut and Lemon Verbena Panna Cotta, 162
Coconut Whipped Creme, 38
Gluten-Free Raspberry Coconut Bars, 96
Thai-Infused Tapioca Pudding with Spiced Mangoes, 170
Oil, about, 16
Okinawan Sweet Potato–Haupia Pie, 34
Tropical Fruit Pie, 118

Coffee "Jell-O" with Coconut Whipped Creme, 38

COOKIES
Almond Thumbprint Cookies, 151
Birdseed Bars, 141
Chocolate-Dipped Macaroons, 26
Cranberry–Chocolate Crunch Cookies, 140
Crispy Rice Squares, 143
Date and Macadamia Nut Bars, 113
Gluten-Free Graham Crackers, 81
Gluten-Free Lilikoi Bars, 92
Gluten-Free Raspberry Coconut Bars, 96
Gluten-Free Peanut Butter Thumbprint Cookies with Guava Jelly, 90
Macadamia Nut Shortbread Cookies, 41
Meyer Lemon Cheesecake Squares, 93
Peppermint–Chocolate Chip Cookies, 49
Pine Nut and Orange Cookies, 159
Ultimate Chocolate Supreme Cookies, 95

CORNMEAL
Awesome Cornmeal Pancakes with Sugar-Free Fruit Purée, 132
Cornbread, Gluten-Free, 80
Polenta Rolls, 65
Pine Nut and Orange Cookies, 159

COUSCOUS
Couscous, about, 16

Orange Couscous Cake, 169
CRANBERRIES
    Cranberry–Chocolate Crunch Cookies, 140
    Cream Cheese–Maple Icing, with Gluten-Free Pumpkin Spice Cupcakes, 82
Crispy Rice Squares, 143
Crunchy Hand Salad with Tasty Vinaigrette, 145
Crustless Broccoli–Cheddar Quiche, 129
CUSTARD
    Eggless Cup Custards, 55

D

DATES
    About, 24
    Date and Macadamia Nut Bars, 113
    Medjool dates, about, 17
    Quick Apple–Date Sticky Buns, 67
    Sugar, about, 24
DOUGHNUTS
    Baked Doughnuts, 37
DRINKS and SMOOTHIES
    Chocolate Mocha Milkshake, 153
    Fruit Smoothies, 133
    Original Sunrise Smoothie, 121

E

Easy Lemon Tiramisu (GF), 100
Eggless Cup Custards, 55
Eggless Oat Muffins, 48
Eggnog Pudding, 53
EGGS
    About, 46-47
    Bird's Nests, 139
    Crustless Broccoli–Cheddar Quiche, 129
    Egg substitutes, about, 46-47
ENERGY BARS
    Birdseed Bars, 141
    Flax Energy Bars, 128
    Gingery Fruit and Nut Bars, 127

F

Flan, Pumpkin, 173
Flax Energy Bars, 128
French Toast, Raspberries and Cream, 54
Fresh Fruit with Vanilla–Ginger Dip, 148
Frittatas, Mini Vegetable, 50
FROZEN TREATS
    Frozen Banana Bites, 154
    Melon and Mint Sorbet, 120
FRUIT
    Almond Panna Cotta with Tropical Fruit Confetti, 28
    Banana–Mango–Macadamia Nut Muffins, 68
    Black Fruit Tart, 110
    Blueberry and Lemon Cobbler, 112
    Blueberry Sauce, with Gluten-Free Pancakes, 97
    Blueberry Slump, 136
    Fresh Fruit with Vanilla–Ginger Dip, 148
    Frozen Banana Bites, 154
    Fruit Kanten, 123
    Fruit Parfaits with Yogurt, 117
    Fruit Smoothies, 133
    Fruit Summer Rolls with Mint and Lime, 116
    Gingery Fruit and Nut Bars, 127
    Healthy Applesauce–Spice Cake, 107
    Mango Clafoutis, 161
    Melon and Mint Sorbet, 120
    Monkey Fruits, 130
    Original Sunrise Smoothie, 121
    Pineapple–Mango Slump, 143
    Pine Nut and Orange Cookies, 159
    Quick Apple–Date Sticky Buns, 67
    Quick Morning Glory Muffins, 70
    Raspberries and Cream French Toast, 54
    Strawberry Gelatin Cake, 104
    Strawberry Ricotta Pizza, 60
    Strawberry Shortcake, with Oat Biscuits, 69
    Sugar-Free Fruit Purée, with Awesome Cornmeal Pancakes, 132
    Tarte Tatin, 115
    Tropical Fruit Pie, 118

G

Garden Tacos, 135
GELLED DISHES
    Coffee "Jell-O" with Coconut Whipped Creme, 38
    Fruit Kanten, 123
    Strawberry Gelatin Cake, 104
GINGER
    Vegetables with Ginger-Garlic Hummus, 149
    Gingery Fruit and Nut Bars, 127
GLUTEN-FREE
    Alternate flours, about, 76
    Birdseed Bars, variation, 141
    Gluten-Free Anadama Bread, 77
    Gluten-Free Banana Bread, 85
    Gluten-Free Carrot Cake, 88
    Gluten-Free Chocolate Pudding Cake, 89
    Gluten-Free Chocolate Spice Cake, 87
    Gluten-Free Cornbread, 80
    Gluten-Free Graham Crackers, 81
    Gluten-Free Mango Bread, 85
    Gluten-Free Pancakes with Blueberry Sauce, 97
    Gluten-Free Peanut Butter Thumbprint Cookies with Guava Jelly, 90
    Gluten-Free Pumpkin Spice Cupcakes with Cream Cheese–Maple Icing, 82
    Gluten-Free Lilikoi Bars, 92
    Gluten-Free Raspberry Coconut Bars, 96
    Magical Bread, 79
    Meyer Lemon Cheesecake Squares, 93
    Olive Oil Lemon Cupcakes with Lemon–Basil Syrup, 160
    Pine Nut and Orange Cookies, variation, 159
    Ultimate Chocolate Supreme Cookies, 95
Graham Crackers, Gluten-Free, 81
GRANOLA OR GORP
    Mango–Banana Mac–Nut Granola or Gorp, 144
GRAPES
    Black Fruit Tart, 110
Guar gum, about, 17

GUAVA
    Gluten-Free Peanut Butter Thumbprint Cookies with Guava Jelly, 90

H

Haupia Pie with Okinawan Sweet Potato, 34
Hawaiian Vanilla Bean and Pear Soup, 165
Healthy Applesauce–Spice Cake, 107
Herb Braided Bread, 62
Honey, about, 24

K

KANTEN (Agar-Agar)
    Agar-agar (kanten), about, 16
    Coffee "Jell-O" with Coconut Whipped Creme, 38
    Fruit Kanten, 123
Key Lime–Avocado Pie, 166

L

LEMON
    Easy Lemon Tiramisu, 100
    Lemon–Basil Syrup, for Olive Oil Lemon Cupcakes, 160
Lemon Verbena, about, 16
LIME
    Fruit Summer Rolls with Mint and Lime, 116
    Key Lime–Avocado Pie, 166
    Sugar-Free Lime–Tofu Pie, 30

M

MACADAMIA NUTS
    Date and Macadamia Nut Bars, 113
    Macadamia Nut Shortbread Cookies, 41
    Mango–Banana–Mac Nut Granola or Gorp, 144
Magical Bread (gluten-free yeast bread), 79
MANGO
    Banana–Mango–Macadamia Nut Muffins, 68
    Gluten-Free Mango Bread, 84
    Mango–Banana–Mac Nut Granola or Gorp, 144
    Mango Clafoutis, 161
    Pineapple–Mango Slump, 143
    Thai-Infused Tapioca Pudding with Spiced Mangoes, 170

Maple syrup, about, 25
Margarine, about, 16
Melon and Mint Sorbet, 120
MINT
   Fruit Summer Rolls with Mint and Lime, 116
   Melon and Mint Sorbet, 120
MOCHIKO
   About, 17
   Azuki Bean Mochi Cake, 40
Molasses, about, 25
Monkey Fruits, 13
MUFFINS
   Banana–Mango–Macadamia Nut Muffins, 68
   Eggless Oat Muffins, 48
   Quick Morning Glory Muffins, 70
Mung bean threads, about, 17
Musubi, SPAM™-less, 146

N

Near East Manapua, 64
No-Bake Cheesecake, 105
No-Bake Pumpkin Pie, 33
No-Egg Salad, 51
NUTS
   Banana–Mango–Macadamia Nut Muffins, 68
   Date and Macadamia Nut Bars, 113
   Gingery Fruit and Nut Bars, 127
   Macadamia Nut Shortbread Cookies, 41
   Mango–Banana–Mac Nut Granola or Gorp, 144
   No-Bake Pumpkin Pie, 33
   Pine Nut and Orange Cookies, 159

O

Oat Biscuit Strawberry Shortcake, 69
Oat Biscuits, 69
Okinawan Sweet Potato–Haupia Pie, 34
Olive Oil Lemon Cupcakes with Lemon–Basil Syrup, 160
Orange Couscous Cake, 169
Orange Yogurt Scones, 73
Original Sunrise Smoothie, 121

P

PANCAKES
   Awesome Cornmeal Pancakes with Sugar-Free Fruit Purée, 132
   Pancakes, Gluten-Free with Blueberry Sauce, 97
PANNA COTTA
   Coconut and Lemon Verbena Panna Cotta, 162
PAPAYA
   Original Sunrise Smoothie, 121
PASSION FRUIT
   Gluten-Free Lilikoi Bars, 92
PEANUT BUTTER
   Crispy Rice Squares, 143
   Flax Energy Bars, 128
   Frozen Banana Bites, 154
   Gluten-Free Peanut Butter Thumbprint Cookies with Guava Jelly, 90
Peppermint–Chocolate Chip Cookies, 49
PIES and TARTS
   Black Fruit Tart, 110
   Chocolate Pudding Pie, 36
   Key Lime–Avocado Pie, 166
   No-Bake Pumpkin Pie, 33
   Oat Pie Crust, 111
   Okinawan Sweet Potato–Haupia Pie, 34
   Sugar-Free Lime–Tofu Pie, 30
   Sugar-Free Pumpkin Pie, 31
   Tarte Tatin, 115
   Tropical Fruit Pie, 118
PINEAPPLE
   Pineapple–Cream Cheese Frosting, with Carrot and Spice Cupcakes, 101
   Pineapple–Mango Slump, 143
Pine Nut and Orange Cookies, 159
PIZZA
   Strawberry Ricotta Pizza, 60
Polenta Rolls, 65
Protein powder, about, 17
PUDDING

Chocolate Pudding Pie, 36
Eggnog Pudding, 53
Gluten-Free Chocolate Pudding Cake, 89
Pumpkin Flan, 173
Thai-Infused Tapioca Pudding with Spiced
    Mangoes, 170
PUMPKIN
    Gluten-Free Pumpkin Spice Cupcakes with
        Cream Cheese–Maple Icing, 82
    No-Bake Pumpkin Pie, 33
    Pumpkin Flan, 173
    Sugar-Free Pumpkin Pie, 31

Q
Quick Morning Glory Muffins, 70

R
Raspberries and Cream French Toast, 54
ROLLS
    Polenta Rolls, 65
    Whole Wheat Rolls, 61

S
SALADS
    Crunchy Hand Salad with Tasty Vinaigrette, 145
    No-Egg Salad, 51
SALSA
    With Garden Tacos, 135
    With Bird's Nests, 139
SCONES
    Orange Yogurt Scones, 73
Sesame Biscuits, 72
SLUMP (cooked dumpling dessert)
    Blueberry Slump, 136
    Pineapple–Mango Slump, 143
SORBET
    Melon and Mint Sorbet, 120
SOUP
    Hawaiian Vanilla Bean and Pear Soup, 165
SPAM™-less Musubi, 146
Splenda, about, 25
Stevia, about, 25

Strawberry Gelatin Cake, 104
Strawberry Ricotta Pizza, 60
Strawberry Shortcake, with Oat Biscuits, 69
Sucanat, about, 25
Sugar-Free Banana Snack Cake, 43
Sugar-Free Fruit Purée, 132
Sugar-Free Lime–Tofu Pie, 30
Sugar-Free Pumpkin Pie, 31

T
Tahini, about, 17
Tarte Tatin, 115
Thai-Infused Tapioca Pudding with Spiced
    Mangoes, 170
TIRAMISU
    Easy Lemon Tiramisu, 100
TOFU
    Chocolate-Dipped Macaroons, 26
    No-Egg Salad, 51
    SPAM™-less Musubi, 146
    Sugar-Free Lime–Tofu Pie, 30
Tropical Fruit Pie, 118
Truvia, about, 25

V
VANILLA
    Fresh Fruit with Vanilla–Ginger Dip, 148
    Hawaiian Vanilla Bean and Pear Soup, 165
VEGETABLES
    Crunchy Hand Salad with Tasty Vinaigrette
    Crustless Broccoli–Cheddar Quiche, 129
    Garden Tacos, 135
    Vegetable Frittatas, Mini, 50
    Vegetables with Ginger–Garlic Hummus, 149

W
Whole Wheat Rolls, 61

X
Xanthan gum, about, 17

Z
Zest, citrus, about, 17